Brief Lives:
Stendhal

Brief Lives:
Stendhal

Andrew Brown

ET REMOTISSIMA PROPE

Brief Lives
Published by Hesperus Press Limited
4 Rickett Street, London sw6 1ru
www.hesperuspress.com

First published by Hesperus Press Limited, 2010

Designed and typeset by Fraser Muggeridge studio
Printed in Jordan by Jordan National Press

ISBN: 978-1-84391-913-1

Contents

S.F.C.D.T.S.V.T.M.B.A.

Hide your life.

Epicurus

Hide your life.

Stendhal

Hide your life.

Flaubert

Brevity is the soul.

Polonius

Since everyone has their own fixed opinion about Napoleon, this Life will completely satisfy nobody.

Stendhal, Life of Napoleon

Do you really want to know Michelangelo? You need to turn yourself into a citizen of Florence in 1499.

Stendhal, The History of Painting in Italy

Preface

This short biographical sketch omits almost any reference to the works of Stendhal. Instead, it focuses on a few anecdotes from the life of Henri Beyle, the man behind the pseudonym 'Stendhal' (though some have claimed that 'Henri Beyle' was actually a pseudonym for the real-life Stendhal).

Beyle brought to the darkening complexities of early nineteenth-century European life (Napoleon; imperialism; industrialisation; the apparent consolidation of European society into the warring camps of bourgeoisie and proletariat) the clarity and powers of analysis that he had learned from largely seventeenth- and eighteenth-century models. He promoted Romanticism but deplored its effusive excesses. His poetry was rooted in coolness and detachment. He aimed at the truth about life, and indulged in mystifications that turned the road to truth into one long detour. But I will not be indulging in literary criticism: this mini-biography is basically a companion piece to *On Love*, and to *Memoirs of an Egotist* and *Letters to Pauline*,[1] and I have not repeated too much of what is already to be found in those works.

In his novels, Stendhal would describe a character and then, twenty pages on, re-describe that character as if meeting him or her for the first time. Despite consistencies of personality, repeated trends and leitmotifs in his life and work, Stendhal is different in everything he writes. 'We shall never be done with

Stendhal,' wrote one of his admirers: this is because Stendhal was always starting out all over again. Hence the freshness of his work, a series of perpetual new beginnings.

His outlook on life was prescient – so much so that its full import is being realised only now, 200 years after he went hunting for ducks in Brunswick, as Napoleon and Goethe were sharing their thoughts on German literature (the most advanced of its time). However, Beyle was writing in the first half of the nineteenth century. So, in spite of his wariness towards the most powerful politician in the France of the 1830s, François Guizot, later celebrated for his encouraging motto '*Enrichissez-vous!*',[2] there are, of course, no allusions in Beyle's work to the contemporary crisis in capitalism,[3] nor – despite his frequent polemics against bankers and industrialists – to the apparently uncontrollable forces of production, accumulation, and consumption that drive the world.[4]

Nietzsche thought that Goethe's work was in itself a whole civilisation. Beyle, on the other hand, was criticised for 'flippancy' by no less than *The Edinburgh Review*. Stung by this, he nonetheless knew that, through a haze of false trails, red herrings, disinformation, sardonic quips, off-the-cuff remarks, fake bonhomie, and strange stories that are either unfinished, or deeply enigmatic, or both, he too was presenting an idea of civilisation, what a civilisation was and what it might be. Of course, the society he indirectly points to (fragmentary, momentary, precarious, intimate) might not be to the taste of more than a small number of people, and Club Stendhal is harsh in its exclusions. *Tant pis.*

'Vinegar is nice, but, when mixed with cream, it makes a perfectly horrible meal,' said Beyle. His works are a pistol shot announcing that the concert is about to begin.

Stendal

The truth, the harsh truth.
Stendhal

The small town of Stendal may be regarded as one of the prettiest in Saxony-Anhalt. Founded by Albrecht 'the Bear' (or 'the Handsome'), who may have died there in 1170,[5] the town, some eighty miles to the west of Berlin, is distinguished by its fine gothic cathedral. The two surviving city gates in brick, and the elegantly gabled town hall, are also noteworthy. Though people often travel through it in a hurry to reach Berlin or Magdeburg, a thoughtful tourist will linger in this modest but attractive township, with its market, its statue of the hero Roland, its fire-brigade museum, and its psychiatric rehabilitation clinic.[6] Like so much of what is now known as 'Germany', it has been located at various times in many shifting political structures. It was part of the March of Brandenburg in the Holy Roman Empire, and a significant member of the Hanseatic League; the new maps of Europe that were drawn after the rise and fall of Napoleon left it situated successively in the Free State of Prussia, the Second Reich, the Weimar Republic, the Third Reich, the German Democratic Republic, and the Federal Republic of Germany, where, at least for the time being, it remains. It is celebrated far and wide as the home town of Johann Joachim Winckelmann, the father of art history (born here in 1717); his deep love of the art of antiquity led him to declare, 'The one way for us to become great, perhaps inimitable, is by imitating the ancients.' Winckelmann went to Rome, and became an expert in the city's sculpture and architecture. He even converted to Catholicism, though cynics have claimed that this was merely to gain access to the Pope's library. It was on his way back to his beloved Italy after a depressing stay in Germany that, putting up at a hotel in Trieste, he was murdered by his bed-mate, Francesco Arcangeli, who coveted the medals that had been given to Winckelmann by the Empress Maria Theresa. There are signs of what the French call a *sale affaire*. But his hometown has honoured him with a Winckelmann Museum, which contains many displays on Johann's life, as well as on classical archaeology and local history.

Stendal is also celebrated for providing Marie-Henri Beyle with his most famous pseudonym, give or take a silent 'h'. Beyle pronounced 'Stendhal' *à la française*, to rhyme with *'scandale'*. He warned that the recipient of a letter from him was bound to be 'Stendhalised' (and scandalised) by its contents. Beyle enjoyed re-inventing names at whim, whether they were those of beloved women (Clémentine Curial became 'Menti'), of towns he lived in ('Rome' became 'Mero'), or of the people he had to deal with (French Minister Guizot became 'Zotgui').

Stendhal – that is, the writer bearing this *nom de plume* – was officially born in 1817, since it was in this year that Marie-Henri Beyle (b. 1783) first used the pseudonym 'Stendhal' in a published work (*Rome, Naples and Florence in 1817*). Why did he choose 'Stendhal'? 'Every year I go to Italy, which is why I once took the name "Stendhal",' he explained. There were probably other reasons, too: perhaps it was because he had been stationed in Stendal during the Napoleonic Wars; or rather, had passed through the town during his time in Germany; or rather, during his stay in Brunswick, a hundred miles or so away, had seen the name on a map and liked it. Or else it was an *hommage* to the town's favourite son, Winckelmann. However, he did not really admire Winckelmann: in fact, he disagreed with his eminent forebear in the field of art history about almost everything. The German scholar's tastes were too Hellenistic, too classical, too frigid, too pedantic – and his works were a congeries of facts and opinions without any real thesis. Beyle noted in his diary, in January 1812, 'Poor Winckelmann: he might have known a lot, but he doesn't argue his case at all well.'

So Beyle may have derived his most famous and enduring pseudonym from a town he barely knew, and whose most celebrated citizen he spent a lot of time arguing against.[7]

There was also, in the 1810s, a 'real' Count de Stendhal (or Stendahl). He was from Sweden, and lived in London. But little else is known about him, except that he was occasionally asked about his exploits in Russia. Perhaps *he* was the real origin of Beyle's writerly name?

Stendhalia

STENDHALIA: an imaginary continent in which
beautiful sopranos sing passionate songs of freedom
while dark young men climb ladders precariously leaning
against lofty towers looking towards distant mountains.
Étienne Braunschweig, 'An Atlas of Utopias'

'*Stendhalie*' is a term used by French writer Julien Gracq to refer
to the world awaiting the reader who 'pushes open the door of
one of Beyle's books'. We can adopt the term 'Stendhalia' to
refer to the amalgam of real and imaginary geography found
in Beyle's works. He was a great traveller, in France, the Low
Countries, Italy, England, Germany, Russia, and (briefly) Spain.[8]
He was an ethnologist forever on the alert for difference –
different climates and customs, different women, different styles
of pursuing life and liberty, etc., different ways of falling in love,
different kinds of art and architecture. The voyager, sensitive to
every nuance, sooner or later melded into the salon *causeur*,
with his anecdotes and maxims and bluff generalities ('the
German language resembles the clucking of geese'; 'all English
women are redheads'; 'Russia is composed of mile upon mile of
empty steppe-land with the occasional fine palace'), and his
desire to entertain at least as much as to inform.

When crossing the border into Stendhalia, even into its
apparently more factual regions (travel writings, art history,

musicology, etc.), the reader is advised to leave any desire for total accuracy behind. Mérimée pointed out that, when editing his works – or, as he often did, completely rewriting them from scratch – Beyle contrived to introduce a new mistake for every one he corrected. Stendhalia, as Braunschweig suggests, can often seem like a fantasy land populated by paper-tiger despots and romantic freedom-fighters, tyrannical father-figures and rebellious *jeunes premiers*, Good Mothers and impulsive prima donnas, stiff, stuffy bourgeois bores and amiable, worldly-wise, mildly heretical priests. Its territory includes lofty mountains (the Alps) and fertile plains (Lombardy), towers and dungeons, places which exist (the brooding, sinister Spielberg prison) and others which do not (the brooding, sinister Farnese Tower in Parma). The western borders of Stendhalia lie in America, a country he never visited (he would have died, he claimed, though at different times he was tempted by Philadelphia and Louisiana), where the price of democracy was that the vote of a Jefferson counted for no more than that of 'the coarsest worker', where the dollar was 'god', and the Protestant work ethic (one of Beyle's particular *bêtes noires*) ruled every hour of the day. (Worst of all, in America, there was, he claimed, *no opera*.)[9] And, in the east, it petered out on the banks of the river Moskva, to which Beyle had accompanied the *Grande Armée* in the campaign of 1812. To the north it extended up to the Shetland Islands; to the south it barely extended much beyond Naples into a hazily surmised Sicily. But Stendhalia, as well as being a realm of mask and metamorphosis, of insistent mythical patterns, of symbols that mock their own symbolic status and yet still signify ('Napoleonic' birds of prey, colours that signal – or do they? – passion and death, ominous presages and dark superstitions that could have come from the world of opera), and of metaphorical networks (mountains, ladders, falls, towers, cells, disguises) that override historical specificity, is also one of the best maps of early nineteenth-century Europe that we have.

Pseuds' corner

He do the police in different voices.
T.S. Eliot

'Stendhal' itself is only one of about two hundred or so pseudonyms adopted by Marie-Henri Beyle (some scholars have counted at least another hundred). The inventive profligacy of his *noms de plume* is partly the result of his hatred of the *nom du père* – a savage reaction to his cold, stingy father. Was Henri Beyle the most pseudonymous writer in history? Here is a very partial list of his aliases (here comes everybody):

Adolphe de Seyssel; A.L. Capello; A.L. Champagne; Alex de Firmin; A.L. Féburier; Alfred de Ch…; Baron Brisset; Choppier des Ilets; Clapier et Cie (a whole firm?); Baron Ddormant; Baron Boudon; Baron Chagrin (in the 1810s he longed to be a baron, but his father never gave him the wherewithal); Chinchilla; Conickphile; Cornichon; Curiosité; de la Palice-Xaintrailles aîné; Dimanche; Fabrice del Dgo (short for 'Dongo'); M. Darlincourt; Dominique (a name he often used of himself in his diaries – probably calqued on the first name of his beloved composer Domenico Cimarosa); H.C.G. Bombet; Fudger Family (a whole family? Did he know what the word 'to fudge' means in English? Did he have a sweet tooth?); Georges Simple (brother of Simon?); Henry Brulard (as in his most protracted essay in autobiography, *The Life of Henry Brulard*); le Léopard (the Leopard);

l'Ennuyé (how romantic); Old Hummums; W. Sterne Renown (he greatly admired Sterne); Favier; F. Brenier; P.F. Piouf; Polybe Love-Puff (partly based on the character Puff, in Sheridan's *The Critic*)[10]; J.B. Lorimier; Octavien-Henri Fair-Monfort; Timbuctoo; Robert frères (a company? a circus act?); Smith and Co. (the commoner names make good pseudonyms); Tavistock (a square as yet innocent of psychoanalysis); Tempête; Timoléon Gaillard; Van Eube de Molkirk; Count Anders von Westwerb (oddly Heideggerean); William Crocodile ('the disguise, I fear, is thin'); and Sphinx. He used pseudonyms even in his letters to his beloved sister Pauline; some he used in more public circumstances; but oddly enough, all these pseudonymous writers wrote in much the same way.[11]

Mérimée thought that pseudonymity was adopted by Beyle as a result of police surveillance. Beyle also regularly falsified the place from where he was writing, pretending, for instance, to be in Versailles when he was *alibi*. He pretended to be describing Holland when he was really talking about France. For periods at a time, he dated his letters to a month or so before he actually wrote and sent them. It is quite true that, under whatever regime, this was a society of spies and informers; in both writing and speaking, *le naturel* was hemmed in by considerations of prudence. Fouché, Napoleon's Minister of Police, reputedly knew everything that was said in the salons of Paris; many of the more subversive of those things were said by Henri Beyle. He had to be careful – and the atmosphere of surveillance aggravated his tendency to surround even the most insignificant actions with mystery. He enjoyed his paranoia to the full. There were enemies everywhere: if they attacked a pseudonym, they were not really attacking him. And he could always fall back on his civil identity if 'Stendhal' (etc.) started to be too uppity. Stendhal might be taken in for questioning, but he could always be released on Beyle.

HB

Well, kid, there are more things in this life than you can
possibly imagine.
Hal Ashby

He tolerated the name 'Beyle', or preferably 'de Beyle', in
official life (the least important part), but it seems unfair to call
him by a surname he rejected. 'Beyle' was often transformed
by his friends into 'Belle', by antiphrasis, since he was neither
handsome nor especially feminine.[12] He himself connived with
this, becoming 'Mr Bell', especially on his English sojourns. He
loved to pretend he was someone he was not. He would even
order work from his tailor or boot-maker under an assumed
name, or allow them to spell him as 'Bel, Bell, Beil, Lebel, etc.'
This could lead to frequent imbroglios. He could hardly complain, either, if his onomastic metamorphoses led to administrative problems, though even at the best of times other people
seem to have been stricken by name-blindness when he was
around. On 16th February 1810, he was obliged to write to the
Duc de Massa pointing out that the 'Reyle, son of the mayor of
Grenoble' appointed as *auditeur* was in fact himself. He added
a copy of his birth certificate to prove that he had been born on
16th January 1782.[13]

Calling him 'Henri' sounds a little too cosy, if not downright
impertinent.[14] His friend Mérimée wrote a short memoir of

Beyle eight years after the latter's death, called simply 'HB', published anonymously. Its *petits faits vrais* [sic] were largely responsible for initiating a long process of mythification. HB is a good name: we can use it as a monogram to keep its bearer at arm's length, distinct from the Great Writer Stendhal who will be present here only as a horizon. HB is the 'singular' individual behind the plurality of the pseudonyms. HB is also associated with pencils containing hard and black graphite (an allotrope of carbon named after its usefulness in writing).

Childhood

The child is father to the man.
Wordsworth

On the feast of the epiphany, 1831, HB wrote:

I have written the lives of several great men: Mozart, Rossini, Michelangelo, Leonardo da Vinci. It was the kind of work that I found most enjoyable. I no longer have the patience to look for materials, to weigh up contradictory accounts, and it occurs to me I could write a life whose events I know really well. Unfortunately, the individual is actually quite unknown: myself. I was born in Grenoble on 23rd January 1783…

The decidedly modern and anti-clerical HB duly came into this world in the street of old Jesuits – rue des Vieux-Jésuites (no. 14: not open to the public), later renamed, not the rue Henri Beyle, or even the rue HB, but the rue Jean-Jacques Rousseau, because Rousseau stayed there in 1768. Here, between Rousseau and the Jesuits, born free but soon in chains in this dark and gloomy house, HB spent his earliest years.

Grenoble was the capital of the Dauphiné, traditionally a region inclined to independence. The Dauphin (whose standard bore as its emblem a dolphin) was the heir to the kingdom of

France: a son, not a father, a Prince Hal rather than a King Henry. Grenoble was not at all noble, in HB's view, but dingy and pokey, with narrow streets and narrow-minded inhabitants. Visitors throughout the nineteenth century commented on the stench of the alleyways and courtyards: the former were used as public urinals, the latter for defecation. It was watered by the greyish Isère and the yellowy Drac. In his letters HB often preferred to call his native town 'Cularo', which at first looks like a typical Beylian code-name (*'cul'* = 'arse') but is in fact historically accurate, being the name of the settlement in which the warlike Allobroges had established a military camp in the time of Julius Caesar. As far as HB was concerned, the best thing about Cularo was the view looking away from it: at least he could lift up his eyes unto the hills.

Not far from his own dark birthplace ('a hundred steps away', he says in *The Life of Henry Brulard* – he had no doubt counted them more than once), at the corner of the place Grenette and the Grande-Rue, on the main square with its well, and the all-too-familiar hustle and bustle of a typical provincial market, was the house of his maternal grandfather, Dr Gagnon: light, spacious, airy, looking south and towards the sunset. In a portrait, Gagnon is full of face, smiling amiably, with a twinkle in his eyes and an eighteenth-century *perruque*. Though a Voltairean (he had travelled to Ferney and brought back a bust of Voltaire) he had also welcomed the anti-Voltaire, Rousseau, to Grenoble. He often treated his poorer patients for free.

Part of Gagnon's property adjoined a terrace that had once formed a section of the old Roman wall: from here, across the town park, the eye could travel northwards towards the mountains of the Vercors. Dr Gagnon watered the flowers on this terrace twice a day; HB would help him, and listen as his grandfather told him about Linnaeus and Pliny, and imbued him with a lifelong passion for meteorology. HB would forever remain sensitive to effects of light and shade, to the changing patterns of the clouds, to sunrises and sunsets, to the stars. Like his master

Montesquieu and his disciple Nietzsche, he was a firm believer in the influence of geography and climate on psychology and politics.

Romain Gagnon was HB's Good Uncle, the son of Dr Henri. Pleasure was everything for him; money counted for nothing. HB used to enjoy watching him don his *robe de chambre* every evening at nine o'clock before supper. And one of the boy's happiest memories was of an excursion with Romain and his wife to Les Échelles,[15] out in the Savoy landscape. Dr Gagnon also had a daughter, Séraphie Gagnon, a Bad Aunt: a harridan, a Catholic and a royalist. She took the child HB on long walks, which bored him; he claims she hated him. How malicious names can be – his father's name was 'Chérubin', and here was a 'Séraphie': neither of them seem to have displayed the virtues associated with their respective angelic orders. HB called Séraphie a 'female devil' and suspected his father of entertaining amorous thoughts towards her after the death of HB's mother.

HB's younger sisters were Zénaïde (a telltale, he said) and Pauline, who later alleviated her melancholia by dressing as a man (unlike her brother, she was unable to escape from the tedium of provincial life). Pauline was more than a sister: she was a *confidante*, a fellow 'passionate' soul, and for many years HB wrote letters to her from all over Europe, filled with warmth, wit, frankness, and tenderness. They are almost as interesting as the mordantly dry administrative letters he sent to army generals and civil service bureaucrats, letters with a strain of suppressed wit and a just-perceptible air of semi-detached sarcasm. (His love letters – at least those that survive – are, like most love letters, dull, with the occasional poignant exception.[16])

From the age of ten, according to his cousin Romain Colomb, HB showed 'an ardent temperament' – brash, untamed, instinctual: but he was fettered by family and fuelled by burning resentment of people from whom he expected affection, most notably his father. He learned to hide himself, to bottle himself up; he hardly ever overcame a basic mistrust; when he did, he was capable of intense friendship, but he remained prickly and easily disappointed by minor derogations from the code of *Beylism*, at which point he would withdraw into his carapace of sarcasm. His father ensured that he was given a very sheltered upbringing: as a result, by the time HB was fourteen, he knew only three or four people of his own age.

Father and son

There are no good fathers: that's just the way it is […]
There is something rotten about the paternal bond.
Jean-Paul Sartre

His mother Henriette died in 1790, aged twenty-eight or thirty (according to HB),[17] in childbirth. HB had adored her. Her favourite reading was *The Divine Comedy*; she also read Tasso. This was uncommon reading material for women: perhaps the association of 'Italy' and 'the maternal' in HB's mind derived from this.[18] He abhorred his father for interrupting the caresses of mother and son: 'I wanted to smother my mother with kisses, and for there to be no clothes […] I loved her; if I ever see her again, I'd still tell her so.' He almost suffocated with grief at the funeral service in the parish church of St Hugues. 'I have never been able to look calmly at that church of St Hugues and the cathedral adjoining it. Merely the sound of the cathedral bells, even in 1828 when I paid a visit to Grenoble, made me feel a dull, dry sadness, without any tenderness, a sadness bordering on anger.' The young HB, forced to endure priestly bromides ('this is God's will'), started to say bad things about this mother-stealing God. His father too was inconsolable, but just looked uglier than ever, his eyes swollen with tears, his body racked with sobs. He took consolation in religious devotion, and contemplated taking holy orders. He locked his dead wife's room; nobody was permitted to enter it until 1798, when he grudgingly allowed HB to set up a table and study maths there, since it was sheltered from the noise of the world. Equally grudgingly, HB admitted in the quasi-autobiographical *Life of Henry Brulard* (written nearly half a century later) that 'this sentiment on my father's part does him a great deal of honour in my view, now that I think of it.' But from childhood on, he disowned his father by calling him 'the bastard': in French *'le bâtard'*, not just *'le salaud'* – he was claiming that his father was illegitimate. HB also loved to speculate on his own possible illegitimacy: his mother *must* have had a fling with someone more handsome and red-blooded than Chérubin? Either way, in classical family-romance style, the line of paternity was broken (as happens in both *The Red and the Black* and *The Charterhouse of Parma*, whose heroes may not be the sons of their 'legal' fathers).

The Abbé Raillane, the tutor chosen by Chérubin Beyle for his children, was feared and detested by his charges. He was 'small, skinny, very pinched, with a green complexion, lying eyes and an abominable smile' – and, worst of all, 'a dry soul'. When, as a writer, HB strove to repress his innate expansive lyricism and to write 'dryly', he was on one level identifying with the aggressor. The Abbé saw danger everywhere, and sneered at the local children who went swimming in the river. If only they knew how dangerous it was. They might drown while not in a state of grace! Raillane tried to teach HB to dissemble his true feelings – 'You mustn't say what you feel, it's not *the done thing*,' he told the boy – a lesson his pupil learned only too well, while also loathing the hypocrisy that such dissimulation entailed. HB later took as a motto *'Il ne faut pas être "comme il faut"'* – 'never do "the done thing"'. HB took particular umbrage at the Abbé's insistence on continuing to teach the Ptolemaic system long after Galileo, because, said the Abbé, 'It explains everything and in any case it is approved by the Church.' HB could not believe the stupidity and mendacity this involved.[19] While France was freeing itself from at least one kind of tyranny, HB remained under the tutelage of this sinister domestic despot until the summer of 1794.

Aux armes, citoyens!

… in that dawn to be alive…
Wordsworth

The French Revolution broke out on 7th June 1788 – at least in Grenoble, where a scuffle involving an old woman 'revorting' (*sic* – her pronunciation) against repression, and a worker suffering a fatal wound, marked a definite heightening of already seething political resentments. A year later, in Paris, the Bastille fell. The new republican authorities in Grenoble decided to channel the revolutionary fervour of the local youths into 'Companies of Hope', which would parade up and down in the Jardin de Ville, overlooked by Dr Gagnon's terrace, with drums beating and rifles shouldered. HB, still a young boy, gazed at this martial spectacle with longing. His father forbade him to join. So HB wrote a letter to his grandfather, signed *Gardon* (the name of an ardent local Jacobin and defrocked priest), asking Dr Gagnon to send HB to the *temple décadaire*, formerly known as the Église Saint-André, where children were being enrolled in one of these republican battalions. But the forged signature was recognised by a hunchback called Tourte who taught HB and his sisters arithmetic and writing. This forgery was probably not HB's *proton pseudos*, but it shows how early he learned the arts of disguise. His punishment was relatively mild: he was sentenced to dine alone for three days. Colomb claims that in the 1790s, HB and he cheered the successes of the republican armies while still sharing 'the royalist opinions of our parents', but these opinions were soon replaced by fervours of a different sort. News of the execution of Louis XVI was brought on the mail coach from Lyon one evening in January 1793; HB's father was distraught, HB was filled with joy. Chérubin Beyle was actually imprisoned for a while, for failure to adhere fully to the new revolutionary regime. HB told the family at large that his father did not love the Republic sufficiently, and fully deserved his spell in gaol. But having a father in prison planted a seed in his mind that later produced enigmatic fruit.

HB was distraught by a different death later that year; that of his boyhood friend, Dr Gagnon's personal valet, Lambert. The 32-year-old valet had died after falling from a ladder while gathering mulberry leaves for his silkworms. Silk, a ladder, a fall: an oddly poignant constellation of details. Lambert had been an intelligent man, and had befriended HB at a time when the latter had few intimates. Aunt Séraphie scolded HB for taking the death of a mere servant so hard.

Contre nous de la tyrannie...

> Without well-educated citizens, the Republic cannot
> flourish.
> *Decree of Year III*

At the behest of Revolutionary authorities in Paris, Écoles
centrales were opened in the main town of every *département*,
to replace the old schools run by the Church. Dr Gagnon, who
had already played a major role in setting up the public library
in Grenoble, was involved in organising the new school. HB
listened as his grandfather gave the opening speech on 21st
November 1796. He was overjoyed to be free of the Abbé
Raillane: but his new comrades soon found him haughty and
sensitive, 'Spanish', *different*, while he found them boorish and
filled with 'egoism'. At school, and later in the army, he would
find friendship only after an initial period of alienation and distance. At school he learnt science, drawing, and logic. He would
always love '*la lo-gique*' at least when pronounced with his own
Beylian drawl: '*la lo-gique*' was the royal road to happiness, and
enabled him to spot hypocrisy in others and contradictions in
himself. He started to read widely in French and foreign literature – Shakespeare and Addison, Pope and Ossian, Goldoni and
Metastasio. He had already had the run of his grandfather's
library: at the earliest opportunity, he bought the *Oeuvres de
Florian*, and read them in secret with his cousin Colomb. Works

with enticing names such as *Estelle, Galatée, Gonsalve, Numa* inflamed his imagination.[20]

One evening in January 1797, between 7 and 8 p.m., HB, Colomb and ten other schoolmates committed an act of political sabotage. The Arbre de la Fraternité, a pretty lime tree, had been transplanted by the authorities – much to its regret – to the Place Grenette: on it, a painted canvas with the words 'Hatred of Monarchy, Constitution of Year III' was hung. The boys shot at it, and smashed this emblem of republicanism – thereby throwing their families (already under suspicion of being insufficiently revolutionary-minded) into the greatest alarm, and causing fears of a 'vast conspiracy' against the current government, though no charges were brought. The anecdote is of interest: HB, counter-revolutionary? Not necessarily, probably more: HB, enemy (sometimes) of pompous symbols, and lover of trees.[21]

And also lover of girls: Victorine Bigillion, for instance, the intelligent and reflective sister of his friend François. She later remembered HB as ugly, of course, but as clever and charming.[22] After a period of flirtation, he may have cold-shouldered her; she was mentally unstable, and her condition declined.

De la musique avant toute chose

Play on.
WS

As a teenager, HB also became a lover of the theatre, and of music.

He took lessons in violin, clarinet, and singing, but with little success. He blamed his father for leaving his musical education too late, and for not having an ear for music. When HB later set up as an opinionated and entertaining connoisseur, his friends reproached him for his ignorance of the technical side of music. He retorted that, thanks to his innate sensitivity, he could hear things in music to which more learned *mélomanes* were deaf. His talents were always those of sensation.

Aged fifteen, still in Grenoble, he heard the *Traité Nul* by singer and composer Pierre Gaveaux, who had, a few years earlier, written a 'Hymn to the Supreme Being' and a Jacobin song 'The Awakening of the People'. A few years later, Gaveaux would write the opera *Léonore, ou l'amour conjugal*, the plot of which would provide the basis for Beethoven's *Fidelio*, a story of love and imprisonment. In Grenoble, Gaveaux's music was sung in 'a poor faint little voice' by Mlle Kubly. HB fell in love immediately. With Virginie Kubly? Yes. With Gaveaux's music? Probably not: at the time, he found the music dull. With music *per se*? 'Here began my love of music, which has perhaps been my strongest and most expensive passion, it is still there now I am fifty-two, more intense than ever.' He was so overwhelmed by La Kubly that he felt faint whenever her name was mentioned, and ran away from her in the Jardin de Ville; he later deemed the moment when he asked someone where she was staying 'probably the bravest action in my whole life'. But she never learned of his feelings for her.

Mathematics

Everything is number.
Pythagoras

I loved, and still love, mathematics in itself, since it does
not allow of hypocrisy and vagueness, my two pet hates.
Stendhal

On 16th September 1798, 'Citizen Beyle' won the first prize for
Belles-Lettres (or 'Beyle-Lettres') at school. Indeed, he won several
first prizes (one of them was the works of Homer, in the fine
translation by Bitaubé), but from 1798 he became particularly
interested in mathematics. He needed money for extra maths
classes; his Good Aunt Elisabeth (maybe eighty years old as the
calendar goes, but thirty at heart) gave him the necessary cash,
but he had to keep these lessons quiet from his father. His
teacher, a Monsieur Gros, was idolised by HB: he was a poor and
virtuous republican, modest and disinterested. One day, having
heard an important piece of political news, he spent part of the
lesson discussing politics with his class – and then turned down
payment, since they hadn't learned much maths. In addition (so
to speak), that glamorous, inspiring figure General Bonaparte
found mathematics congenial since, in it – the young General
averred – 'all is resolved by logic' and 'all is rational'. As an
artillery officer, Bonaparte had studied mathematics (projectiles,

parabolas, bodies in a state of motion); *ergo* all young men now wanted to go to the great school of engineering in Paris, the École polytechnique: QED. HB duly won first prize in maths, and was presented with Euler's *Introduction to Infinitesimal Analysis*, in Latin. Now he, too, would escape from Grenoble and go to 'X', as the Polytechnique became known (its emblem is a couple of cannons crossed saltire-fashion, though 'x' is also a suitably mathematical symbol).

So, in the last autumn of the last year of the eighteenth century, Chérubin Beyle saw his son into the *diligence* that would take him to Paris. The father's eyes were filled with tears; the son's eyes were dry, and filled with a gleam of anticipation. How happy he was to be escaping Chérubin, and Cularo![23]

Paris

PARIS, world capital of wit!
Valéry

HB arrived in Paris after a journey of six days, on 10th November 1799, i.e. just after 18 Brumaire of Year VIII. Napoleon, returning from his inconclusive campaigns in Egypt and the Middle East, conspired first with and then against the Abbé Sieyès, managing to persuade sufficient people of the dangers of a Jacobin coup d'état to stage one of his own. On 18 Brumaire and the following days, Napoleon effectively destroyed the *Directoire* and replaced it with the Consulate. At one point he apparently claimed, when faced by hostile deputies, *'The Revolution is over.'* Overwrought, tense, haranguing the crowd, at one moment he almost fainted and fell.

Paris was now filled with 'enthusiasm for the hero who, with his mighty hand, had just seized the reins of State', according to Colomb. It is easy to imagine the effect all this had on the mind of HB, arriving from small-town provincial France (all the easier in that he described it several times over). But political fervour was dulled, in his case, by disappointment. 'Paris is full of narrow, muddy streets, dark and dirty.' It was just like Grenoble, only worse. And there were *no mountains*!

He had already more or less abandoned the idea of sitting the entrance exam to the École polytechnique. Instead of studying ballistics, he would study *beylistics*. He held firm to his refusal, despite the encouragement of the Daru family (relatives of his grandfather Gagnon), with whom he was now staying. He ate with them (boring: old man Noël Daru was 'severe'), missed the landscape of the Dauphiné, and had just enough pocket money to buy books on the quaysides. He was always buying books, says Colomb, but often left them behind him when he moved lodgings.

Pierre Daru, HB's cousin, had been appointed as Secretary General for War in Napoleon's new regime. Daru found a job for HB (as 'supernumerary') in his ministry. HB never quite overcame the sense of intimidation he felt in front of this man, who was admired by Napoleon for his zeal and efficiency (he made Daru a Count), and feared by all his subordinates (HB himself could not look at the door of his office without trembling). One day Daru dictated a letter to HB, who spelled *'cela'* as *'cella'*.[24] This mistake enabled Daru to wax ironical. Ha! So much for 'this brilliant humanist who had won all the prizes back home!' HB suddenly felt like a very small fish in a very big stream – and thereafter, partly defiantly, partly out of sheer *désinvolture*, claimed that nobody with imagination ever bothered about orthographical exactitude. (In any case, Daru, who had produced a fine translation of Horace, was prone to similar spelling mistakes. Even Homer nods.)

HB took up art lessons with M. Regnault, whose studio was a room in the Louvre. He soon gave up. He preferred to be a connoisseur rather than an amateur. He loathed the boredom of Sundays (he had not yet been to England, where the *spleen* induced by the tedium of Sabbath observation made even the hardiest of continental visitors contemplate suicide). He felt little kinship for the other men in the office, who (he thought) viewed him as a madman or an imbecile. They used to go and piss against the trees in the office yard, which filled this dendrophile with horror (though he did the same).

Daru took HB to one of the literary societies that flourished in Paris at the turn of the century. HB was horrified by the insipid poetry being quoted – so inferior to Ariosto, and to that great French poet Voltaire! But the occasion was redeemed by the presence of a pretty woman or two – for instance Mme Constance Pipelet, later the Princess of Salm-Dyck, painted with her adorable mop of curly hair sitting in a neo-classical posture in 1797 by Jean-Baptiste François Desoria.

Napoleon (now First Consul) and his Minister for War, Carnot, had long been laying plans in secret for the campaign of 1800 that was to change the map of Europe. The brothers Daru, Pierre and Martial (the latter an easy-going man who helped HB overcome his shyness with women) collaborated on the preparations, which involved assembling, in Dijon, a reserve army of some 15,000 men. The Darus were then ordered to go to Italy. They decided to take the bored, fretful HB with them, even though they were not particularly sure what he would be doing there. HB immediately packed thirty volumes of books in '*éditions stéréotypées*', a neat new invention of which he was particularly fond.

Italy

… Italiam fato profugus…
Virgil

Soldiers! I will lead you into the most fertile plains in the
world. Rich provinces, great cities will lie in your power;
there you will find honour, glory and riches. Soldiers of
the Army of Italy, will you lack courage or steadfastness?
General Bonaparte

HB left Paris in mid-April 1800, travelling to Dijon and then
Geneva, where, ever the *tourist* (a word he helped to popularise),
he hurried to the rue Chevelue to see Rousseau's birthplace, by
then a rather rundown hovel. The crossing of the Mont Saint-
Bernard (accomplished by Napoleon on a donkey, despite David's
later depiction of him on a rearing steed) marked a new era in
HB's life. At the fortress of Bard, he came under fire for the first
time (a virginity he was glad to lose); but Bonaparte showed his
military genius by simply marching round the fort, which was left
to hold out, rather forlornly, behind the French lines. HB, just
seventeen years old, was filled with joy; he could now imagine
himself as all the great literary protagonists he had ever read
about – Don Quixote and Le Cid, or the heroes of Ariosto and
Tasso. But this new recruit almost never made it across the Alps:
he was nearly thrown from the convalescent horse given him by

Pierre Daru when it bolted. (His father, inevitably, had never allowed him to learn how to ride.)

As they continued along their route, HB was taken under the wing of a French captain, a tall, blond, slender man of the world, 'everything that an excellent governor should be for a young prince', but a little too 'dry' for HB, who preferred to go off by himself, daydream, and absorb the vast quantity of new sensations flooding into his soul. From now on, he was always seeking new sensations; he would become hysterically bored if these were lacking. In society, he would react against the ever-present threat of tedium by resorting to sensational paradox and provocation, causing amusement and unease around him. He thought that boredom was always the result of a fundamental mendacity; people lied to curry favour, to avoid humiliation, to pretend they were something they were not. The truth was always bracing. He replaced Kant's categorical imperative with *thou shalt not be bored* (and the even more demanding *thou shalt not be a bore*): an interesting basis for an ethics, and not as flippantly dandyish as it sounds.

In Novara, he ignored the warnings of his Captain ('you're sure to get your throat cut!') and, aware that he was a member of the *occupying forces*, went to the theatre. Here he heard Cimarosa's opera *Il Matrimonio segreto*. This was the greatest epiphany of his life, it gave him a 'divine happiness' – more for the music than for the plot, despite the presence in the latter of a stingy, pompous, and self-important father-figure, Geronimo. HB was even drawn to the actress playing the role of Caroline, one of whose front teeth was missing. 'To live in Italy and listen to this music' became the purpose to which all his thoughts now tended.

Then he was in Milan, a city 'five times bigger than Grenoble', as he told Pauline. Milan rapidly became the capital of Stendhalia: it opened up a whole new dimension in his life. When he thought of Italy, it was essentially as a peninsula that was lucky to contain such a city. When he was forced to leave Milan on campaign, he discovered that he hated *polenta*, and found the Italian peasants brutish and superstitious, even if they were full of vitality. On his return to Milan, at Christmas, the church bells of the city pierced the thick fog with their deafening clangour; he was suffering from a heavy cold, but the carnival season had just started, and the whole city, with its illuminations and masked balls, was transformed into one giant theatre.

In Milan, autobiographical and dramatic ambitions flourished. 'I have decided to write the story of my life day by day. I don't know if I'll have the strength to fulfil this plan, begun already in Paris.' He meditated on the art of drama, and read volumes I, II, III, IV, V, VI, VII and VIII of Laharpe's textbook *Lycée*, though he later decided that Laharpe was an old fogey. He reacted strongly and unpredictably to the art around him, and he could be extremely critical, even of Italian actors: he disliked the Italians' way of performing a drama by Régnier that he saw, and went off to the gaming tables instead. Military duties and periods of leave allowed him to explore other parts of north Italy. From Bergamo he caught sight of the Apennines – but he was not tempted by the two countesses staying in the same Bergamesque lodgings, since they were twenty-eight or thirty years old, and, to his fastidious mind, 'dirty'. Throughout May 1801 he was feverish, and took quinine, as well as a mixture of tamarisk, cassia, and senna that made him vomit. A doctor later told him that his real illness was *ennui*, aggravated by nostalgia and melancholy. But his health was never robust. He had by now picked up a sexually transmitted disease requiring (as they all did) treatment with mercury. He again started taking clarinet lessons with a poor teacher; he studied counterpoint, and quickly translated, with the help of an Italian grammar book, Goldoni's *Zelinda e Lindoro*. He drew up an immense list of books that he had read or hoped to read – English, Dutch (Vondel), Italian, Spanish, and Portuguese. He took an Italian tutor. The fever returned at eleven o'clock every evening. 'Let's make haste to enjoy life, our moments are numbered, even the hour I've spent feeling poorly has brought me closer to death,' he wrote. He jotted down some thoughts – picked up from a fellow soldier – on making love to 'an honest woman'. You get the lady to lie down, and kiss her and finger her a bit until she starts to enjoy it, even though (as custom dictates) she will pretend not to. Then, without her noticing, you contrive to place your left forearm across her neck, under the chin, as if to strangle her. She will instinctively bring up her hand to protect her neck. Meanwhile, you take your prick between the index finger and middle finger of your right hand (both fully extended) and calmly place it in her 'machine'. So long as you keep your cool, it never fails: but remember to distract her attention by making a few little moaning noises.

In his diary he made notes on army manoeuvres, the towns he visited, and the local beauties. Brescia: quite an attractive place, middling size, located at the foot of a low mountain; the prettiest woman here was Mme Calini, and Mme Martinengo was quite easy on the eye as well. Maybe Brescia deserved a couple of stars in the *HB Guide to Stendhalia*, if only because of its eccentric music lovers.[25] And, always and everywhere, his mind recurred to the theatre: he longed to be **'a future young dramatic bard with a future young actress'**[26] (9th February 1805). He continued to be a discerning critic of drama (usually in the privacy of his marginalia) for the rest of his life. Here, for instance, are some of his critical remarks on the dialogues in a 1711 five-act drama by Crébillon *père*, called *Rhadamiste and Zénobie*: 'That's a bloody useless reason'; 'Newspaper style'; 'Obscure and bad'; 'Awful'; 'These tirades are so unnatural'; 'How insipid and stupid!'; 'Poor and badly written'. Even Corneille's *Horace* brought out the Beckmesser, that patron saint of critics, in him: 'That's really bad', he rapped of one line of verse; 'Bad', he hammered at another; 'Very bad', 'Weak', 'Awful'.

Here are some other examples of HB's diary observations:

I will almost always be mistaken when I judge any man to be all of a piece.

Almost all the misfortunes of life arise from the wrong ideas we have about the things that happen to us. To have a thorough understanding of men, and to judge events sensibly, is thus a great step towards happiness.

I must never sacrifice the energy of expression to what is supposed to be good tone.

In October, in the town of Bra, HB drew up a list of the personal effects of Citizen H.-M. Beyle, sub-lieutenant in the 4th company of the 6th regiment of dragoons of the Army of the French Republic, One and Indivisible. As well as listing all his clothes and his weapons (a sabre, two braces of pistols, etc.), he detailed his travelling library, which included twelve volumes of Homer, eight of Molière, and five of Racine, together with Virgil and Horace, Ariosto and Condorcet; Italian, French, and English grammar books; and various military documents and rule-books. Italy was proving in every sense an educational experience.

Theatre

In the art of declamation, breathing is everything: but
a lively eye fixed on your audience will also convey your
passions effectively.

Gustave Maret

Despite the delights of Milan, HB was soon rather bored with
the soldier's life, and resigned his commission. He returned to
Grenoble and then Paris. By the summer of 1802 he was in love
with Adèle Rebuffel, his cousin, whom he sometimes referred to
in later diary entries as 'Adèle **of the gate**' because the family
home was in the rue Basse-Porte-Saint-Martin. She gave HB a
lock of her hair, but told him she was in love with another man.
She was capricious, alternately cold-shouldering him and showing real affection. On 26th August 1802, he kissed her; the following evening, she treated him with indifference. Should he
keep going to see her and her family? He noted in his diary for 1st
August, 'I'm not going to see them.' Then, on 1st September,
'I'm not seeing them.' 2nd September: 'I'm going at 7 o'clock.'
4th September: 'I'm going.' 8th September: 'I'm going in the
morning.'

In the summer of 1803, in Paris, he looked back over the
months he had spent taking lessons in the art of declamation.
He found it difficult to learn his lines, and was hampered by his
timidity, but 'the finest day of my career' was on 21st February

that year, when he played Racine's Oreste to Adèle's Hermione, in front of an audience of twenty-five people. He overcame his nerves and was swept away by his role; everyone was weeping; he felt 'electrified'. The next day, he coughed up some blood. He was trying to live in Paris as a *philosophe*, but was far from philosophical about the measly allowance of 150 francs per month sent to him by his father. He had tasted war and was no longer quite so obsessed by the need to rival the great French general Turenne: instead, he wanted to 'write comedies like Molière and live with an actress'. His room in the rue d'Angivillers looked out over the colonnade of the Louvre; he read La Bruyère, Montaigne, Rousseau (too overblown), Alfieri (at this stage a duty rather than a pleasure), and the *idéologues* (philosophers whose emphasis on clarity of thought, and on paying close attention to one's sensations, impressed him), notably Cabanis, Destutt de Tracy and J.-B. Say. 'I lived solitary and crazy like a Spaniard, a thousand leagues away from real life.' He learned English from an Irish priest; he made good progress; soon he was mad about Hamlet. He was still sexually uncertain. 'I am a strong twenty-year-old and think of myself as having the right constitution for the pleasures of love, and yet I can reduce myself to the point where I no longer desire women at all and discharge, without pleasure, just once a fortnight.'

On 14th June 1803, the anniversary of the battle of Marengo (HB was a great observer of anniversaries both public and private), he drew up a list of people he knew, either personally or because they were in the news: generals, commissioners for war, students of the École polytechnique, bankers, classmates, shopkeepers, and several famous contemporary poets ('Mazoyer, Dalban, Lemazurier, Chazet, Pirard, Cailhava'). About this time his journal starts to resort more frequently to both Anglo-Beylish and Italo-Beylish: on 20th August 1803 he notes, '**A epistle to** Édouard **upon the** ball **of yesterday. This relation shall remember to Marthe the charm of this** nei quali eravamo insieme [in which we were together]. **Her cosin M. F. shall guid**

her imagination.' This seems to be a reference to his friend Édouard Mounier and his sister Victorine (her full name was Marthe-Marie-Victorine), with whom HB promptly fell in love. Still timid, he resorted to giving only indirect signs of his passion, leaving her quite bewildered.

He again visited Geneva. The local preachers were mediocre, but he liked the frankness of the citizens. He thought that, here, he was starting to learn about his fellow humans by observing them rather than just reading about them. On his way back to Paris he stopped off in Lyon and found its architecture 'bizarre' and its women 'ugly'; they had poor complexions and little feet, and were prone to affectation. Back in Paris, he listened closely to the advice of Urbain-Philippe Salmon, a doctor in the Hanoverian Army who had spent seven years in Italy; Salmon was a man whose judgement he could respect. Philosophy was in the air: the Kantian Revolution had started to spread to France, and the cafés of Paris occasionally echoed to the great debates on the *Ding-an-sich* raging on the other side of the Rhine. It was an age of systems, and some of them seeped into HB's notebooks and diaries. After a walk through the Jardin des Plantes, he wrote of his impatience for his papers to arrive from home: 'I can't wait until my trunk of belongings arrives so that I can start working; I'm tired of not being famous.'

One of the great pleasures of Paris life is the ease with which members of the public can wander into lectures given by world-class scholars at the Collège de France. Sheltering from an April shower, HB here listened for a while to Pastoret, professor of Law, expounding Grotius. Sometimes, in the evening, he would go for a walk through the Tuileries with his 'true friend' Fortuné Mante, who had been crucial in introducing HB to the *idéologues*. **'We speack of passions and philosophy.'**

In Grenoble he had started writing a comedy, *The Two Men*; he had already composed 306 lines, and when his trunk finally arrived, at the end of April 1804, he settled down to work. On 11th May he spent eight hours trying to get line 353 right, and failing. By 20th May he had reached line 375. He was producing an average of three lines a day. He had earlier reckoned that each line cost him an average of two hours and fifty-six minutes. He started to loathe the alexandrine verse form, and to equate it with tyranny.

He was also alert to the whiff of despotism he detected in Napoleon's increasing assumption of absolute power. On 15th February 1804 (still officially known as 25 Pluviôse of Year XII), General Jean Victor Marie Moreau was arrested on a charge of plotting against Napoleon. Moreau had helped Bonaparte in his coup d'état of 18 Brumaire, and commanded armies in Italy and on the Rhine. HB wrote a memoir in defence of Moreau, and years later, in 1837, noted that throughout the period 1803 to 1806, he had secretly detested 'the tyranny of the Emperor who was stealing France's liberty'. He even claimed that Mante, his old friend, had involved HB in 'a sort of conspiracy in favour of Moreau (1804)'. His devotion to Napoleon, the only man (he said) whom he admired, could veer into harsh criticism during the (long) period in which Napoleon was essentially a dictator.

If he won the lottery, there were several things he would like to buy (or so he proclaimed in a 'decree' of 5th May 1804 that he drew up for his own personal constitution): a pair of slippers, two new dressing gowns (one in silk), two nice editions of Corneille and Racine... He spent much time in the Bibliothèque nationale, studying authors who, he felt, might help him develop his own style. Goldoni's *Memoirs*, in French, were a good model, and he played with the idea of treating several of Goldoni's subjects in French. Goldoni's *Il Cavaliere di buon gusto* would make an excellent play called *The Man of the World*. Its hero would be a man of taste and wit, who would cope with every difficulty and acquit himself with honour and grace. Replying in advance to all the bores who might rebuke him for plagiarism, HB remarked sagely, '*My* play would have absolutely nothing in common with *his*: he depicts an Italian man of the world in three acts, I'd be depicting a Frenchman in five acts, with a different storyline.' This was, after all, how Shakespeare worked. (But, he noted later, Shakespeare lacked both the *sceneggiatura* of Alfieri, and Corneille's skill at writing verse: if only he'd had these, the English dramatist would have reached 'the height of perfection'.) He continued to read in a predatory way, issuing peremptory judgements on his reading to anyone who would listen, and, if not, consigning them to his diary. Hume was 'mediocre', Vauvenargues 'very mediocre'. He decided that everything of interest to him in Descartes's *Discourse on Method* could be put into three sentences. He continued to meditate his own *filosofia nova*.

On 30th June 1804, M. Daru *père* died. At the house of mourning, HB met his daughter and decided that she had set her cap at him, or rather, in Anglo-Beylish, 'that she had cast her eyes upon me **for a husband**': but he found her rather ugly. The next day he attended the funeral prayers for Daru at the Paris church of St Thomas d'Aquin: the priests looked base, vicious, and stupid.

D.G.A.D.A.A.B.T.

All warfare is based upon deception. Thus, when capable
of attacking, feign incapacity; and when actively moving
troops, feign inactivity.

Sun Tzu, The Art of War

HB constantly used his diary to 'read into my sensations'.
On 12th July 1804 he noted, 'My lack of self-assurance comes
from my habitual lack of money.' The only way to gain any self-
confidence was always to have a lot of money in his pockets. But
how? He blamed his father for not sending him enough to
impress potential mistresses. In January 1805, suffering from a
fever that had lasted eight months, with continual indigestion,
unable to afford decent boots, cold and miserable, he brooded
over his father's irresponsibility in leaving him so morally humili-
ated by poverty that he would have blown out his brains five or
six times over if not for his love of study and his hope of glory.
His father hadn't even replied to his request for an advance. He
drew up an indictment, leaving room for it to be extended at
leisure. 'After all that and twenty pages of details all of them
horribly aggravating, my father is being a *wicked villain* to me,
without virtue or pity. *Senza virtù ne carità*, as *Caroline* says *nell'
Matrimonio secreto.*' HB felt he would be able to write another
fifty pages on the topic, and prove his case against his father
before the six greatest men alive (this tribunal included Georges

Gros – the geometer who had taught him mathematics – Destutt de Tracy, and Chateaubriand).

Never mind: a few days later he was writing, '**Happyness gived by the wether, and mery resignation upon my father's avarice.**' And in February, he was positively beaming, and indulging in the dandyism that would be an inspiration to so many later French writers, from Balzac onwards. He was 'never so brilliant', HB noted, in his 'black waistcoat, black silk breeches and stockings, with a cinnamon-bronze coat, a very nicely tied cravat, and a magnificent shirt-front'. (This from a man who, in his novels, kept his description of wardrobes to a functional minimum.) He looked almost as handsome as the great actor Talma; his ugliness vanished. Dandyism was one of the things that kept his spirits up. It was in March of this year, 1805, that he noted, 'It's my belief that character and strength reside in not giving a damn about a thing – just keep going on.' Years later, in much darker spirits, he invented a motto for himself: D.G.A.D.A.A.B.T., or 'don't give a damn about a bloody thing' (in French: S.F.C.D.T., '*se foutre carrément de tout*' – scribbled, for instance, into a copy of the *Memoirs* of the Duke de Saint-Simon). He engraved a shortened version of this on a mantelpiece back home for his sister to observe, and brandished it in a letter to the great scientist J.-J. Ampère: it was his grouchy version of Rabelais's *Pantagruelism*, which Rabelais characterised as 'a certain gaiety of mind adopted in response to contingent events'.[27]

HB read the papers assiduously, especially the *faits divers*. Near Genoa, a jealous lover had shot dead his beautiful fifteen-year-old mistress out of jealousy; he had fled the scene, written two letters (HB excitedly decided he must read them), returned to his mistress's body laid out in the chapel at midnight, and by the flickering light of the candles turned his pistol on himself. Pure Othello – and further proof that 'sweet Italy [*la douce Italie*] is the land where people have the strongest feelings, the land of poets'. Poetry, passion, and murder: the zodiacal stars of his Italy.

On 14th July 1804, he attended the great parade held at the Tuileries. He could see Bonaparte perfectly well, just fifteen feet away, on a fine white horse, wearing the uniform of a guards colonel. He was greeting everyone, and smiling. 'A theatrical smile,' thought HB, 'the kind where you show your teeth, but you don't smile with your eyes.' This parade actually took place on 15th July, not 14th July;[28] on 15th July, Napoleon went from the Tuileries to Notre-Dame to hear a *Te Deum* and then to the Invalides for a ceremony with the members of the Legion of Honour.

HB often revisited his diary. On 11th August 1804 he noted, 'This month has been spent in the study of high philosophy [*la grande philosophie*] to find a basis for the best comedies possible and, in general, of the best poems, and [...] the best way for me to find in society all the happiness that society can give me.' Never has a man studied happiness more, never has a man had more faith that studying happiness can make you happy. Eighteen months later, on 10th January 1806, in Marseille, he reread this entry and was pleased at the profundity of his self-analysis, though he also thought that the *Logic* of Destutt de Tracy would help him to make it even sharper.

On 12th August 1804:

This notebook [i.e. a separate notebook HB started to keep on this day] is getting off to a happy start, today, Sunday 24 Thermidor; having taken for the first time an extract of gentian and a *tisane de petite centaurée et de feuilles d'oranger* [a herbal tea made of centaurea and orange flowers], I am as happy as possible, at three o'clock in the afternoon, sunshine after rain, discovering the fine thoughts which can begin my notebook on *firmness of willpower*. [He dedicated his notebook to willpower and Frederick II.] It's a happiness of a gentler kind, but just as strong as on that Sunday in Claix[29] where, after writing the first good poetry I had composed in my life, I dined alone, quite at ease, with excellent spinach in juice and some nice bread. Given man's nature, these ecstasies cannot last.

All of HB is here: the happiness of memory and anticipation, the desire to write a book on willpower (rather than the need to manifest the willpower that would enable him to complete a book on willpower), and the mixture of sensual and intellectual delights (he later wrote that his only enduring tastes had been the Duke de Saint-Simon and spinach). His happiness now mingled with the feelings he had experienced when his lovely cousin Adèle had leaned against him during a firework show (of which he seems to have attended a great number).

On 28th August 1804, he wrote that Molière's glum 'misanthrope', Alceste, 'ought to see that all the ills he cannot endure come from monarchical government, and should turn the hatred that he feels for the vices of his contemporaries against the tyrant'. Depression is a political matter – a symptom that, somewhere, there is a tyrant lurking.

On 16th November 1804, he was again in the Bibliothèque nationale, reading some autograph letters from French King Henri IV to his mistress the Marquise de Vaudreuil. 'They [the letters] charm me, that's the right word for it; it's in them that naivety [*la naïveté*] should be studied, just as much as in La Fontaine. Study naivety? Yes; when, as yesterday, I don't feel very well, when I have good ideas and feelings too, my soul studies naivety, learns to feel it.' Three days later an instruction to himself: 'Listen to, and follow, the natural [*le naturel*] in my conduct and my style.'

On 9th December 1804 he wrote an account of Napoleon's coronation the previous week. At the last minute, in Notre-Dame, Napoleon had taken the crown from the Pope and placed it on his own head – but this gesture of imperial autonomy was not enough for HB, dismayed at the kitsch of it all, and aghast at the Emperor's need to have the (reluctant) Pope there in the first place. 'I reflected a great deal throughout the day on this blatant alliance of all the charlatans. Religion coming to consecrate tyranny, and all in the name of men's happiness. I rinsed my mouth out by reading a little of Alfieri's prose.' But the 'illuminations' at the Tuileries were very fine. Still obsessed by Victorine Mounier, he drew sketch maps of the salons in which he encountered her: so many battle plans, with lines for manoeuvre, formations to adopt for a first skirmish, and corridors down which he might safely retreat. He celebrated Christmas Day 1804 by going to a brothel.

He was starting to grow more confident in expressing his views, sometimes in a direct and forthright way, sometimes ironic and ambiguous. A brief self-portrait of 14th January 1805 shows how he imagined he appeared to others:

> My noble republican principles, my hatred of tyranny, the natural impulse that leads me to see through hypocrites, the imprudence with which I say what I can see in their souls, and the energy they can see in mine, the natural and sometimes ill-disguised impatience that I feel for mediocrity, all lead feeble souls like my uncle [Romain Gagnon] to think that I am a Machiavelli. What they call a Machiavelli is, in their view, the most terrible of animals. Superiority arouses their most irreconcilable hatred.

This 'superiority' made his bonhomie and frankness seem less attractive and led to difficulties even with friends. 'These are all the unpleasant things that a *great* and *virtuous* soul, formed in solitude, without communication, must endure when it enters society.'

His superiority did not always extend to relations with women, where any pose of *donjuanisme* rapidly crumbled into bashfulness and diffidence. His diaries were soon brooding over a new question: should he sleep with 'Louason'? This was his name for the actress Mélanie Guilbert, his latest *amour*. Ignoring the fact that she might or might not want to sleep with him, he listed the disadvantages. 1) Pacé was just about to have her, and she had told Pacé she had the clap, or someone else had told him; either way, she knew Pacé knew she had it; 2) she probably did have the clap; 3) she would probably want to be paid, and HB didn't have the money. If only his father…

14th March 1805. 'I feel that she [Mélanie] occupies my whole soul. I have no sensibility left to feel anything else. Everything I do is done mechanically; my thoughts are always fixed on her, she is always in my mind's eye, and, since my experience prevents me from confiding in anyone, I can find relief only in writing.'

At the end of March 1805, there was a party at the home of Mlle Duchesnois, the actress (he called her 'Ariane'), which he described over eleven pages of his diary, inspired by his love for Mélanie: 'I have fire in my veins.' But then we hear what will be a refrain in his autobiographical writings and diaries: 'I'm no longer writing down my charming memories, I've realised that this spoils them.'

At the beginning of April, HB told Mélanie, in her bedroom, that he would follow her to any part of France she chose. He would abandon everything for her, he would help look after the daughter she had from a previous liaison. She was so moved that she had to turn her head to the window to hide her tears, and then asked for her handkerchief. It wasn't in her room, and he had to go into the living room to fetch it: 'I did not dare dry those charming tears away myself.' With a little more self-assurance (or a little less love) he might have had her there and then.

She moved to Marseille, and he followed her, finding a job in an import-export company. In a hotel, on 25th July 1805, he and Mélanie finally became lovers. He was soon trying to communicate to her his own passion for the *Logic* of Destutt de Tracy.

Half of his ambition had now been realised: he was living with an actress. But the other half – to be the greatest dramatist since Molière – was proving less easy; his job as (essentially) a clerk and errand boy was not enough to satisfy his ambitions;

and there were soon tensions between himself and Mélanie, who departed for Paris in the spring of 1806. HB was left to mull over his isolation and his sense of being, yet again, stuck out in the provinces. On 23rd April 1806, he confided a night of morose delectation to his diary. In a doorway illuminated by a streetlight in Marseille, he had fingered up the local whore Rosa. At midnight he went to her place, and at 1 a.m. they had sex. He was soon dying from disgust. He did it to her twice, he made her do it six times. He went off, feeling ashamed and depressed, at 6 a.m. 'Bugger her,' he thought, gloomily – yes, he might go back and do just that. As his beloved Shakespeare put it: 'Before, a joy proposed – behind, a dream.' He soon returned to Paris, and pursued an increasingly desultory relationship with Mélanie.

After Trafalgar, the Napoleonic regime was becoming increasingly paranoid; theatres were closed, newspapers kept under surveillance, censors and spies were everywhere. It was difficult for HB to discover what was happening outside an increasingly claustrophobic hexagon. But he soon had a chance to find out for himself. On 6th August 1806, the Holy Roman Empire was dissolved (illegally) by its last Emperor, Francis II. Napoleon's empire was bellying out eastwards. And there were jobs for the boys. On 23rd August 1806, HB noted, 'I'd been really hankering after a post as *auditeur*;[30] I go to court, but the sight of so many embroidered men in posh clothes who don't seem particularly happy really puts me off.'

On 1st September 1806 HB went on a pilgrimage to Rousseau's hermitage in Ermenonville, near Paris. A local woman referred to the great writer as *Janques*. (On a later visit, HB reflected that Rousseau could have been the Mozart of the French language if only he had been able to abstain from pedantry. Rousseau had preferred to be the 'legislator' of mankind rather than simply entertaining it.)[31] HB was charmed by the great chestnut trees, but found the hermitage itself, with its house and its garden, commonplace. He suddenly felt lonely in the midst of his travelling companions: he had spotted a flirtation going on between two young people (their guide, a boy of sixteen, and a plain-looking ten-year-old girl with rotten teeth), and tried to draw his companions' attention to this rustic *amour*, but they took no interest in his remarks. He longed for more sensitive friends who would appreciate and share his 'tender and delicate thoughts'. That night, moonrise was an odd, slightly uncanny affair: the moon rose red in the sky, cut across by slate-coloured clouds. That evening he again slept with Mélanie; the following day he felt fed up and weary, perhaps because she had been telling him of her previous life and loves.

Napoleon set off for the Diet of Frankfurt. He was unsure whether to reopen hostilities with his potential enemies beyond the Rhine: but he did want to 'put the wind up them'. Some of his *chasseurs*, convalescing in the École militaire in Paris, jumped out of the windows to follow him: and HB too was suddenly devoured by ambition and restlessness. He listened, yet again, to *Il Matrimonio segreto*, and sensed that he was starting to get a feel for the harmony. But he felt trammelled and indecisive; he was bored, and boring. Luckily, he was able to follow the Daru brothers yet again – this time, to Germany.

Germany

But where is Germany? I can't find it anywhere.

Johann Wolfgang von Goethe and Friedrich von Schiller

Germany still did not exist as a political entity; its mosaic of statelets and princedoms was coming increasingly under the heel of Napoleon's Army of Liberation. Some Germans welcomed Napoleon – he would shock Germany out of its late-mediaeval, feudal patchwork into a modern, enlightened, and unified state. On 14th October, Napoleon won the Battle of Jena: Goethe had his wedding ring engraved with that date, considering that it marked a new epoch in his (and everyone else's) life; Hegel, notoriously, had seen the Emperor, 'that World Soul', riding through the small university town on his way to the battlefield, and Heine too resorted to cliché, ironic or not, when he spoke of the Emperor's 'eternal eyes set in marble' and 'the calm of destiny' that he manifested. HB entered Berlin with the Emperor on 27th October 1806, pistols loaded and cocked, or so he 'remembered' thirty-four years later (he also remembered being present at the Battle of Jena, which was not true from the standpoint of mere empirical understanding or *Verstand*). He played his part among the occupying forces with his usual efficiency. In Brunswick, he was sent to survey the great Wolfenbüttel Library that had been built up during the Thirty Years' War; he was a little lax in this task, preferring to acquaint himself with the locals. His colleague, Vivant Denon, was meanwhile paying a visit to Goethe; the Frenchman was organising the confiscation of many of the art treasures of Europe, now destined for the Musée Napoléon – a truly imperial act of cultural pillage. The wily Goethe persuaded him there were no artistic pickings to be had in Weimar.[32]

Germany now provided a third term for HB to triangulate with France and Italy. The country he duly annexed to Stendhalia was a region of tender melancholy whose inhabitants, sometimes dreamy, sometimes boorish, grunted in an unamiable language[33] and wrote unreadable philosophical gibberish, but could often be rather pretty. HB had a largely imaginary affair with 'Minette', full name Wilhelmine de Griesheim. She was, in his words, 'the younger daughter of a penniless general who was the ex-favourite of a fallen prince'. (The penniless general was in fact disgraced and sent into exile at the end of 1807.) She was already engaged, but HB told her he had fallen madly in love in with her. Would she still receive him after her marriage to M. de Heerdt? 'Certainly,' she replied (he wondered whether she was being coquettish) – and added that she wouldn't be married for a long time yet. (In fact, her fiancé was killed during the Napoleonic Wars.) He bided his time, and explored the surrounding areas. On 23rd June 1807, he visited Gross-Twülpstedt, some twenty miles away from Brunswick, and on the journey enjoyed a cold collation of cake, butter, and chocolate, with rum and *Bischof* (a sugared wine flavoured with lemon or orange). Minette and her fiancé went with him; despite his jealousy of Heerdt, HB found his rival (a Frenchified Dutchman) to be a man of good sense, if a bit plain and platitudinous, and plied him with questions about Holland. HB also noted how a German fiancé or husband never left the side of his (future) wife, spoke to her constantly, was 'intimate' and affectionate: something that would seem shocking in Paris. Indeed, he was taken aback to discover that it was customary in Germany to marry *for love*. This was surely a sign that the Germans were less civilised than the French? The latter at least refused to allow romantic love to upset social conventions: the German way of paying court was positively *indecent*. HB, as he mellowed, would nuance this harsh view in *On Love*: indeed, he was soon forming a more judicious view of the Germans in general. They had, after all, produced the two greatest sovereigns of the eighteenth century, Frederick II and Catherine II.[34] But the Germans were cold and heavy; they lacked character, and their literature lacked style (though he was quite impressed by four of Schiller's plays that he read in French translation: he was bound to be attracted to this tyrannicidal playwright). They were inclined to legalism and formality, they spent too much time reading the Bible (like the English); maybe it was the fault of German food (black bread, butter, milk and beer: they needed a good, strong wine to liven up their sluggish muscles). But they showed remarkable trustfulness: they were even prepared to send money through the post.

On the morning of 1st July 1807, HB sang a duet from *Il Matrimonio segreto* with a certain M. Denys. Two days later, after many 'detours', he managed to relieve his boredom by pinching the thighs of Mlle d'Oehnhausen. His hand even managed to wander up to 'the place where the ebony starts to shadow the lily'. But he was already bored with Brunswick, and sought amusement by buying a black dog that he called Brocken, after the celebrated and magical mountain. The dog was stolen a few months later. Like Goethe, like Heine, like Frederick Wilhelm I of Prussia and his queen Louisa, like so many other celebrated tourists, HB made the ascent of the Brocken, and stood on its summit surveying the scene – the plains, the forests of Thuringia, the view towards Gotha and Weimar, as well as the flat lands of Brunswick and Hamlin. He found the visitors' book to be full of platitudes (what did he expect?).[35] He seems to have been ignorant of, or indifferent to, the spectral associations of the Brocken: no *Walpurgisnacht*, no Faustian witchcraft, thronged his literary memories. Cured of his love for Minette, he started having sex regularly (every three or four days, just for physical reasons) with Charlotte Knabelhuber. 'I was pleased with myself in this respect,' he noted in his diary, of one encounter.

In the early summer of May 1808, he was out on horseback when he saw a house on fire in the plain below. Aware of previous mishaps with skittish mounts, he at first hesitated to gallop down to investigate. In a letter to Pauline, he drew a little sketch-map, explaining that he had thought the hill sloped down towards the fire at a very steep angle: but he had overcome his fears and ridden down. Reflecting on his own still occasionally hesitant character, he mused on the great souls of antiquity: Brutus, whose name he had carved on his desk, and Regulus. He thought they were imbued with 'a noble simplicity'; they were like tragic heroes, sublime: '**I think that I shall have this in my character.**' He dined at the Prefect's, and went hunting (for hare and ducks), and dancing. On 6th March 1808 he watched as the people of Brunswick swore an oath to the new political status quo, and noted that, in Germany, an oath was sworn by holding up the first two fingers of the right hand, palm outward. He meditated on the possibility of writing (or of someone's writing) a 500-page '*history of the Catholic religion*, from Jesus to our own day' – one that would be perfectly impartial. He decided that peas were a 'sovereign remedy against love'.

On 14th October 1808 he noted that Napoleon had just granted an audience to Goethe in Erfurt. They had spoken together of German literature. This was the famous occasion on which the Emperor remarked admiringly to his entourage, '*voilà un homme!*' HB concluded that monarchs had this advantage over common mortals: they were surrounded by the best people of their time. He was currently preoccupied by writing a *History of the Spanish War of Succession*: yet another of his projects that remained unfinished.

Vienna

You will find me at six o'clock at the Blue Ox, if I am not
out walking in the Prater, under the chestnut trees.

Beethoven

Then came a brief interlude back in Paris, where, in 1809,
HB started learning Spanish, and translated three pages of
Don Quixote. 'Spanish lesson, dancing lesson, bath, dinner, read
Crébillon *fils* with pleasure' (8th February 1809). In a footnote
added in 1813 he added, 'This is merely a diary meant for my
own self-observation, of no interest for other people.' He also
added, 'Out of prudence, not knowing where to put my papers,
nothing political, all names changed.' Then he was off to the
wars again, on Napoleon's Vienna campaign.

HB crossed the Rhine on 12th April 1809. The river was
low, and the sun was shining after a rainstorm. His pleasanter
memories of Germany were reawakened, especially when he
saw a pretty girl at a window in Kehl. 'Time may change my
ideas, but everything I like about Germany always assumes the
shape of Minette.' He noted the obtuseness and obstinacy of
the peasants and the beauty of the gardens. On the way to Ulm
he decided that the landscape was, especially under the rain,
rather austere. He mulled over 'psychological considerations
and vainglorious feelings', and caught a cold.

19th April 1809 was a day 'fertile in sensations'. In Burgheim, he and his companions saw the German regiments of the Confederation of the Rhine (dragooned into submission by Napoleon) massacring a gaggle of geese with their sabres. He was greatly amused by the spectacle. A little later, he caught a glimpse of the Danube between two hill-slopes: the landscape was one of the most beautiful you could imagine, except for the fact that it lacked mountains and a lake. He thought he heard cannon-fire in the distance and his heart leapt with pleasure: but alas, it was merely thunder.

In a wayside inn he ate an excellent fricassee. There were three pretty girls there, except that one of them wasn't all that pretty, another was even less attractive – she had the figure of an angel (if, that is, angels have big bottoms), but her face was terribly pockmarked – and even the most alluring of them had a 'fluxion'. But HB noted that his imagination made up for any superficial defects in their appearance: overcoming his 'bashfulness' (a word he often used in English, abbreviating it, in his algebraic way, to its initial letter '**b**'), he laughed and joked with them for a whole hour. 'The illusion I feel is the same as that I derive from a theatrical performance.' His soldiering was carried out under the severe eye of the choleric Pierre Daru, who was in a hurry to catch up with the Emperor: HB was convinced that Daru (who constantly called him 'a scatterbrain') would never really like him. The town of Landshut in Bavaria was captured by General Mouton; HB saw a burned bridge which had seen action on the previous day; the bodies of three '*kaiserlich*' soldiers were still lying there, the first he had seen on this campaign. Landshut reminded him of Italy; its women had lovely oval faces. Here he helped out in the local chaotic hospital (with just one Austrian surgeon), giving a hand to the wounded as they were unloaded from the wagons, and feeling quite useful. At night he and his fellow soldiers would sleep in uniform, in case they were attacked by the enemy. Occasionally, he felt like having one of the women who ran the local taverns, but generally he didn't have the time or the inclination. The fields were full of discarded shoes, caps, and the wrappers of cartridges. When forced to travel at night, HB and his fellow officers would occasionally doze off on their horses' backs and awake with a start to discover that their mounts were galloping down some steep slope. Sometimes it was difficult to find lodgings: there was swearing and yelling, the rain came tumbling down, the locals spoke no French. But then, against the background of the smoke rising from the campfires of the bivouacs outside a town while dark figures passed to and fro in front of the glow, there would be a young mother to brighten the scene, surrounded by children with their fingers in their mouths, staring in wonder at this stocky young Frenchman as he turned on the charm and sought shelter for himself and his fellow-officers. Occasionally, art enlivened his weary eyes: even a bad copy of a lovely Madonna by Guido Reni that he found in one of his lodgings cheered him up.

In Lambach, in Upper Austria, there was a terrible fire; HB was always a great observer of fires and, even though one officer was badly burned, he mused on the beauty of the spectacle. 'A column of smoke filled with light drifted sideways across the town, it lit our way for a good two leagues.' As he advanced, the piles of dead (both soldiers and horses) increased. He scrutinised the expression on the charred and disfigured faces of the dead. One German soldier on the bridge at Lambach had died with his eyes open: 'Courage, fidelity and German goodness were visible on his face, which simply expressed a certain melancholy.' When the carriage in which HB was travelling had to roll over these corpses, he felt sick. He later learned that the battle for the bridge had exacted maybe 1,500 deaths; many soldiers had been burned alive.

Napoleon was meanwhile subjecting Vienna to a sustained bombardment. Beethoven stayed in the city, even though he feared that the constant din of cannon-fire would ruin the last shreds of his hearing[36] and moved down to the basement of his house, clutching pillows round his head to protect his ears.

He was glad he had cancelled his dedication of the 'Eroica' to Napoleon: the liberator had become a warmongering petty tyrant like all the rest. Beethoven was more preoccupied by the departure from Vienna of his friend and patron the Archduke Rudolph, and, in his basement, worked at the first movement ('Farewell') of a piano sonata in E flat major.

By May, HB too was in Vienna, where he was placed in charge of the imperial hospitals. Félix Faure paid him a visit there and was impressed by the care with which the pale, moustachioed French soldiers were treated, and the cleanliness and good order of the wards (much better than in most hospitals in France). HB, adopting a stiff and distant demeanour to hide his shyness, took a real interest in the sick and wounded, who were provided with branches to wave away the flies that buzzed through the hot summer air.

In June HB was writing to his sister Pauline to congratulate her on not, after all, being pregnant – she should make the most of her freedom from motherhood and gallivant about a bit, see Milan, Genoa or Berne (not such an easy thing for a married woman with an improvident husband). As for him, though he was forced to assuage his loneliness by reading Thomas Gray's 'The Deserted Village',[37] he was still enjoying the social life of Vienna ('riding, women, and divine music') on the rare occasions when he could escape from his work. On 5th–6th July, stretched on a *chaise longue* and suffering from headache and impatience (a fever had laid him low), he listened to the cannon-fire coming from only five miles to the east of Vienna. He wished he could be there, with Daru and the Emperor. The wish was father to the deed, and HB later claimed that he had indeed fought at Wagram.[38] He had seen Napoleon on the battlefield, he later lied, in his *Life of* and *Memoirs of Napoleon*, in which he claimed to be 'brave enough to tell the truth *about everything*'.

He travelled into Hungary and admired the chestnut trees; he also admired the handsome Croatian soldiers (moustaches, and silver-trimmed little boots, rather like French hussars). Back in Vienna, in the Schottenkirche, he attended the funeral of Haydn, a composer whom he did not altogether like – but who would soon come in useful. From his pew in the second row, HB, in uniform, dispassionately observed the female mourners from Haydn's family in the row ahead of him: dressed in black, they had mean, pinched faces. Mozart's *Requiem* was played ('too noisy'). When he was suffering from fevers and frets both real and emotional (he was unhappily in love again), only Cimarosa's *Matrimonio* could console him. 'The effect of the music of the *Matrimonio segreto* is to make me find fewer obstacles to everything (it increases the sanguine element in my temperament).'

In November 1809, HB went to see Emperor Francis II attending a service of thanksgiving at St Stephen's cathedral. HB was in civvies and wearing a bizarre opera hat he had managed to salvage from somewhere (French uniformed officers were too conspicuous in the streets and often attracted animosity from the populace). He observed Francis, a small, slender man with a vacant face, doffing his three-cornered hat under the gusts of snow. The crowd uttered ecstatic cries of '*Vivat!*' 'I thank you, my children,' the affable monarch paternally replied. HB managed to make his way into the crowded cathedral: the Emperor, drenched to the skin from the snow, seemed even slighter and more insignificant than he had looked outside. HB was recognised as 'one of those Frenchies' by whispering voices on all sides: but it was all worth it, since he caught sight of the Raphaelesque Madame Salmi, the most beautiful woman in town, and complimented her on her appearance. He spoke a little too loudly; everyone turned to look. But he was shivering with cold and wet: even though the choir was just embarking on a fine *Te Deum*, he went home to get warm.

He was by now in love with his boss's wife, Mme Daru ('Madame Z.'), who had come to accompany her husband on his official duties. On one occasion she needed to leave the city with M. Daru; before she left, HB played with her gloves as she sat on a sofa waiting for her carriage to arrive. She asked for the gloves back, but – he was convinced – her voice had a certain tenderness. He kissed her hand, and when she stepped into her carriage, she said, 'Adieu, my dear cousin,' and kissed him goodbye – surely with an unusual degree of feeling?

In Linz, at half past midnight in the early hours of 1st January 1809, he paused by the banks of the Danube to listen to the distant drums and trumpets, trying to remember where he had been on previous New Year's Days.

Happ

Happiness is a new idea.

Saint-Just

Napoleon left Vienna; Archduke Rudolph returned; Beethoven was able to complete his piano sonata, with movements called 'Absence' and 'Return'. It is one of the most Stendhalian celebrations of love and friendship in all of music. In January 1810, HB visited the salt mines of Hallein, near Salzburg, where he observed the phenomenon of crystallisation, in which crystals of salt form on a branch thrown down into the depths; he would turn this into a metaphor for falling in love, in which the imagination builds delicate but durable structures around some contingent and even commonplace encounter.

In February 1810, back in Paris, HB became preoccupied again by ambition, in this case by the desire to be appointed *auditeur*. He enjoyed the spring weather and Mozart (*Figaro* – he thought he might fall in love with Mlle Mars singing the role of Susanna). On 2nd March 1810 he noted, '*A day full of happ.*' Happiness? Happenings? No: just **happ**. HB started to plan a history of the French Revolution. He was often bored. Emerging from one social occasion he yawned so much he almost gave himself indigestion. He started to analyse his boredom, reflecting that with just a little 'political genius', i.e. 'the art of attaining one's aim with the elements at one's disposal', it should be possible to convert even the dullest *soirée* into something much more agreeable. After all, everything had been present on this occasion to make an enjoyable evening: 1) youth; 2) wit; 3) beauty; 4) health; 5) financial comfort (*aisance pécuniaire*); 6) experience of the world. But the 'insipid habit of dignity' spoiled everything. In a French village, everyone would have just let their hair down; in Germany, they'd have had a jolly good time; in Italy, everyone would have submitted to the gentle laws of pleasure; but *Paris corruption* (by which, as usual, HB meant vanity: the hankering to show off, the need not to appear an imbecile, the need to police one's tongue and one's thoughts) had spoiled everything. Another name for this drawback in the French character was '*tatillonnage*' – not 'tittle-tattling', though it looks like that word, but a mixture of niggling and meddling, 'an extreme attention and self-important vanity brought to bear on the slightest little details', a kind of social pedantry. Now that he had lived in Italy and Germany, he could cast a critical eye on France. Was French 'wit' really so appealing? He later reflected that his own wit had made him many enemies. And 'the great **drawback** of being witty is that you have to gaze fixedly at the semi-halfwits who surround you, *and imbue yourself with their insipid sensations*'. There was something condescending about even bothering to be witty.

He increasingly used his diary to jot down conversations, invent dialogues, and hone aphorisms that he would then draw on in less overtly 'personal' works – his novels, travelogues, and studies such as *On Love*. This work was crystallised by the greatest and most painful of his *amours-passion*, but he was already accumulating experiences and observations that would help to bandage the singularity of his suffering in general swathes of anecdote and observation. It is perhaps best described in HB's own words (in a letter of October 1833): 'This book is a monograph on the malady [or illness: *maladie*] known as *Love*. It's a treatise on *moral* [or psychological, or social-anthropological: *morale*] medicine. Nothing is addressed to the senses. The language is severe and philosophical, precisely in order to exclude ideas of idyllic or sensuous pleasure that the title might suggest to some young readers.'[39] Indeed, the text – although it has its delicate pleasures and moments of veiled suggestiveness – is far from libertine. It is about love as an exchange of fantasies rather than as the contact of two epidermises. It is not an *ars erotica*, or even an *ars amatoria*. The love it describes is often unassuaged, enacted at a distance, a courtly ritual of sublimation and renunciation, an occasion for rich melancholy rather than satisfied desires. Sighs matter. Through love he groped his way to a philosophy of love: but love *always already* (to speak the language of the schools) had its philosophical moment. And love (like depression) is a political matter. Some of the best chapters in the book concern the education of women: HB was in favour of this, for the typically Beylist reason that a well-educated woman is better company for a man of wit and sensibility.

He was still in thrall to Mme Daru (now called 'Mme Trautmand' in his private jargon). He felt awkward in her presence (a sure sign of passion), and even went to church to be with her. The sermon wasn't bad, but the preacher tried to imitate the sweet mystic Fénelon, whom HB greatly admired. HB, who had been hoping to be moved to tears (as he usually was by Fénelon), remained dry-eyed, much to his disappointment.

On 30th April 1810, he noted in his diary, under the heading '**Charming evening**', the details of a day spent with friends whom he loved. It had finished with an 'excellent iced punch' – this was 'the nicest evening I've ever spent in Paris'. 'I know full well the secret of the pleasure I enjoyed, but I'm not going to tell it in case I tarnish it.' 1810 and 1811 represented something of an apogee in his career, insofar as HB was now leading the life he had initially dreamed of: lunch in elegant cafés, reading Adam Smith, attending concerts at the Conservatoire, dining at the fashionable Frères Provençaux, going to the theatre, spending the evening in the salon of some society lady (he had planned his witty sallies while strolling up and down in the elegant grounds of the Palais-Royal), and then returning home in the small hours to read a scene or two of *Othello*.

On a trip to the Sèvres porcelain factory in early May, he examined 'the prettiest manufactured object I've ever seen': a round table nearly three feet in diameter with the portraits of almost all the marshals of the Empire, and Napoleon himself in the middle.[40] But he found the sculptures of the Emperor to be mediocre: it needed a Canova or a Thorwaldsen to produce something more grandiose than the simpering figure on horseback that he saw portrayed here. In Versailles, he was struck by the relative austerity of Napoleon's bedroom in the Trianon. Over the next few weeks he went on various trips to the environs of Paris (his job included appraising the imperial furnishings), bemoaned the way he was putting on weight, and, in between bouts of boredom, insisted to his diary that he was, 'in general, **happy**', or (since happiness spills over the boundaries from one language to another), '*Io sono felice.*' He listed 'physiognomies' (based loosely on those of Lavater, who deduced psychology from facial appearance) – tiny little vignettes of his friends and colleagues, and other people he met: all good practice for the comic dramatist he hoped to be (and for the novelist he later became). So he noted 'the stupid, empty face' of his minister, and 'the respectable antiquity of M. de Kalkreuth [Prussian Field Marshal], an old grenadier, vegetating, with a ridiculous dress suit showing his trousers behind – and *what* a big behind!', and the Russian colonel, Count Alexandre Czernitscheff, with his tight-fitting clothes always on the point of bursting open, 'four medals around his neck, with the face of a fatuous young nobleman, forever talking with the politeness of the old French court which the émigrés seem to have grafted onto the courtly life of Petersburg'.

The pen-portraits of the characters in his novels will be more sophisticated than these *croquis*, but similarly concise, seeing a whole history (personal, political) in a face or a word. He wrote every day, without – as yet – any aim other than the vague one of being a great dramatist, or at least a great writer, or at least a writer. And as usual, he wrote on whatever came to hand – on the back of an envelope, on previous diary entries, on a restaurant menu... His marginalia are fascinating, and properly marginal. In the *Works of Shakespeare* he wrote, '*A single course of literature in 6 words. True or interesting ideas expressed clearly. All the rest is superfluous or dangerous.*' It is not clear whether this was a description of Shakespeare's style. In Pascal's *Pensées*, 'The philosophical works of Aristotle, Plato, Descartes, Spinoza, Leibniz are boring poems composed by great geniuses. Only Bacon is still useful.' On a copy of his *Life of Haydn*, more tangentially still, he jotted down a prescription against gout, and noted that belladonna could cure migraine. On his slippers he scribbled down a maxim, '*Un poco di freddo per producer il caldo*' – 'a little coldness to produce warmth'. This was apparently an amorous tactic, roughly equivalent to playing hard-to-get. It seems to have been moderately successful, even when he was not wearing his slippers. He continued to mope over Mme Daru, to flirt with other women, to work at his interminable play *Letellier*, a rewrite of *Tartuffe* (he never completed it, despite working on it in 1806, 1810, 1813, 1830... he even fiddled with it while Moscow burned in 1812). He bemoaned the absence of a mistress (but maybe sex would dissipate the energy he needed to become the greatest dramatist since Molière). He started planning his forthcoming expenses; he was by now sure of being appointed as *auditeur*, despite the vexing slowness with which the authorities were processing his case: he would have two servants and two horses, and needed to budget for dinners, lunches, clothes, accommodation, nights out at the theatre and the opera, books, and prostitutes: 14,000 francs should do it, and he looked forward to travelling in his official capacity for four or five months of the year. Maybe he might even be made a prefect? But did he really want this? It might involve being sent to some undesirable province...

Towards the end of July 1810, this greatest of autodidacts, this eternal student, as intent on moral self-improvement as the young Tolstoy, and forever seizing on every opportunity to learn his trade (of living, writing, loving: *visse, scrisse, amò*[41]), decided that he would meld together a volume of Rousseau's *Confessions* with excerpts from Rousseau's educational treatise *Émile*, bind the result together, write the word 'STYLE' on the back, and fill the first page with 'seven or eight truths that I will read every day as my morning prayer'. (About the same time, Hegel suggested that reading the newspaper might be a good way of replacing the morning prayers of former generations.[42]) He continued to seek guides to the literary life. Who could he learn from? Helvétius, Hobbes and, to some extent, Burke (he had probably not read much Burke yet, but he had seen the name in Hobbes and made a mental *q.v.*). This would be his literary theory. With his passion for concocting endless lists (of friends, lovers, books, items to be purchased, debts, celebrities, self-improving maxims) he decreed that the whole of literature consisted in five principles:

1. 'You cannot depict what you have never seen, nor judge of portraits made by others';
2. 'The sublime, a feeling of empathy with a power that we see to be terrible';
3. 'Laughter (see Hobbes)';[43]
4. 'The smile, the sight of happiness';
5. 'Study a passion in books on medicine (Pinel),[44] in nature (letters of Mlle de Lespinasse),[45] in the arts (Julie, Héloïse, etc.).'

It is noteworthy that HB deemed philosophy and medicine to be important for the study of literature. He added that the 'proof or refutation' of his principles should be sought in Shakespeare, Cervantes, Tasso, Ariosto, and Molière.

He also gave himself maxims to ponder every morning: a kind of *become who you are*, or an *ordre du jour pour le Roi*:

1. '*Te lier davantage*': perhaps to *network*, as we say these days – he owed it to himself '**as bard**', as '**ambitious**', and as '**love-pleasure**' (the same trinity of activities as before: write, live, love).
2. To gain the same tranquillity of soul as Beaumarchais, even amid the most turbulent circumstances.
3. To 'observe ridiculous actions and people without being affected by them'.
4. 'Don't overstep your budget'.

The last would prove the most difficult. In 1813 he added another footnote here, remarking of his maxims, 'That was wise; I see my character more clearly these days'; and, on 21st June 1815 (just three days after the Battle of Waterloo) he footnoted that footnote, 'Exactly true. Instead of loving ambition, I have always been bored stiff by the things an ambitious person is forced to do. Hardworking solitude in the middle of a great city, **good for my happiness.**'

3rd August 1810: 'A remarkable day **in my life**.' He worked from 8 a.m. to midday, met up with Félix Faure and went for a walk, saw a couple of plays and, preoccupied by the thought of the news that might be awaiting him, returned home, asking his concierge offhandedly whether there were any letters for him. A parcel was handed over. He opened it, and read:

The Minister Secretary of State hastens to inform M. de Beyle that he has been appointed *auditeur* in the Conseil d'État, by decree of the 1st inst. He has the honour of forwarding to M. de Beyle the official letters enclosed with his letter of the 1st inst.

Saint-Cloud, 3rd August 1810

HB carefully copied this into his diary and added, 'I opened this welcome letter at twenty-two minutes past eleven o'clock in the evening. I am twenty-seven years, six months and twenty days old.'

And so HB became a fully paid-up member of Napoleon's bureaucracy. In October 1810, he was given the task of overseeing a general inventory of the contents of the Louvre museum, now called the Musée Napoléon; his colleague was Vivant Denon. HB's task included classifying and describing, briefly, all the *objets d'art* in the Imperial collection. His post carried a certain prestige; he could wear his smart white trousers (so attractive to the ladies) with pride. But more important – even – than this was the fact that almost every day he would walk through the Louvre, in which hung so many artistic masterpieces (many of them stolen by the Ogre of Corsica): an artistic training that he eventually put to good use.

The comet

His fate and mine are inextricably linked.

L'russe Besuhov, on the Beast of the Apocalypse, in War and Peace

On 29th January 1811, Angéline Bereyter, a singer at the Opera (HB called her 'Frau Mozart', since she was currently performing as Cherubino), became his mistress. Despite his continued 'bashfulness' in her presence, they enjoyed each other's company – too much? 17th March 1811: 'It seems to me that my physical happiness with Angéline has deprived me of a considerable part of my imagination. **I make that one or two every day, she five, six and sometimes** nine times.' Too many sneezes, too many belly-laughs. On 20th March 1811, he was lying in bed with the sleeping Angéline. At ten o'clock, cannon-fire awoke her: it was the third cannon shot. They counted intently: how many shots would be fired? Twenty, twenty-one... Twenty-two! It was a boy! The Emperor had produced a boy! In honour of the new King of Rome, Napoléon François Joseph Charles Bonaparte, the cannon fired 121 shots (if it had been a mere girl, only twenty-one shots would have sounded). HB shared in the general delight. The Empire seemed secure. Maybe he could use his duties as *auditeur* to take him back to Italy?

On 27th March 1811, he noted rumours of an impending war with Russia.

On 8th June 1811, his thoughts turned to biography:

If I ever had the honour to approach His Majesty, I would suggest that he had his life story written by four authors, working separately. Two volumes for every year, 10,000 francs per volume for the authors. [...] These volumes would be corrected by a commission composed of two people and handed over to the printer's as the work of a single individual, or at least given a print-run of 4,000 copies, and the edition preserved to be published at an opportune moment.

On 10th August 1811 he noted that these days, whenever he had any free time, he was forced to 'have a cup of coffee, shut myself up and

FEEL BORED,

because I have nothing of interest to keep me occupied.' And yet this man, addicted to good company and conversation, also wrote that happiness consisted in being able to retire to your room, alone, and lock the door behind you.

On 25th March of this year French amateur astronomer Honoré Flaugergues, in Viviers, had observed a comet in the constellation now known as Puppis. Over the next few weeks it became increasingly visible to the naked eye. On 6th October, Herschel, in Glasgow, noted that its double tail was twenty-five degrees long; by December 1811, one of the two branches was over sixty degrees in length. It then faded rapidly, and by January 1812 was barely visible: but it had been a naked-eye object for nine months, and a spectacular sight in the night sky. On 31st August 1811, HB observed it in a clear, starry sky at 3 a.m., and did a little sketch of it in his diary. 'It was a kind of pyramid in shape. The distance between its summit – the brightest point – and the end of its rays was the same as that between the last star in the beam [*timon*] of the Plough and the four other main stars.' A little later, the delicate blue light of sunrise reminded him of the dawn scene in Lesueur's opera *Les Bardes ou Ossian* which had been one of the hits of the summer season of 1804. Now he decided that the dawn reminded him of that music (in which he seems, from his 1804 diary, to have taken little interest at the time): in a remark worthy of Oscar Wilde, he noted that the dawn mimicked the music perfectly.

Some observers thought that the comet, travelling with inconceivable velocity through infinite space, portended terrible events: a new outbreak of hostilities, the fall of mighty empires, even the end of the world.

Italy, *da capo*

HB contrived a new trip to Italy, leaving on 29th August 1811.
En route, in Dole in the Jura on 1st September 1811, he again
observed the sunrise, with the blue light of dawn and some sublime clouds. In Geneva, he noted that the moon seemed to be
missing a piece (*écornée*); it had been full when he arrived, and
was again round early the next morning. A chambermaid told
him that at one moment, only a small part of the moon had been
visible. He concluded that he had witnessed an eclipse of the
moon without realising it.

He found the women of Geneva (which he had already visited
twice) to be tall and handsome, with nice figures and complexions, but a little chilly in demeanour, perhaps a touch too serious.
Anyway, however beautiful they might be, recent experience had
made him weary; he and Angéline had grown bored with each
other; their relations had become too regular and bourgeois; 'all
it needed **for expelling love** was **the want of ideas of Ange and
hundred** and twenty **nights ever together'**.

Then he was back, from 7th to 22nd September, in the capital city of his own private realm. A diary entry in Milan, Sunday 8th September 1811, reads, 'My heart is full. Yesterday evening and today I have experienced the most wonderful feelings. I am on the verge of tears.' And, 'I sense in every pore of my body that this country is the land of the arts. I believe the arts hold the same place in the hearts of the inhabitants as vanity does in the hearts of the French.' Two days later he wrote to Pauline, 'It is here that I have loved the most. It is here, too, that my character was formed. Every day I see that I have an Italian heart, apart from the murders – and in any case, people do exaggerate these.' His imagination seized on the city and Stendhalised it. In San Fedele, admittedly a jewel of a church, he even enjoyed mass. (He usually resented church services, which prevented him from enjoying the art and architecture in peace, and forced him to make 'extremely gauche genuflexions' in front of the altar.) San Fedele was hung with scarlet damask, the air was cool and pure. The faithful were scattered along the pews of the church; all of a sudden, the sounds of a 'charming little sonata' filled the space: there was a man playing the organ, with two women. Outside, he noted the 'noble architecture' of the surrounding building, and the cleanliness of the cobbled streets, and thought back to Paris – dirty, stinking, muddy Paris – with distaste.[46]

Social life in Milan was as entertaining as ever. The amiable but insipid Signor Migliorini latched on to HB (who, while not suffering fools gladly, learned as much from them as he could). Migliorini even divulged a 'secret method' for getting an erection. You need a tarantula, which you burn to carbon; you add olive oil and turn the ashes into a paste; then you rub the big toe of your right foot with it. Result: an erection. When you get tired of this 'pleasant state', you wash the mixture off with hot water. This helpful advice was a little vitiated by the 'complete absence of wit' which accompanied its delivery: but Migliorini was, quite unawares, giving HB a useful insight into local mores (for Migliorini showed typical Italian caution in not wishing to try this method out on himself). HB remarked, rather ruefully, that Migliorini was the opposite of HB himself: handsome and healthy, but without wit, *and yet* able to have women.

His impassioned appreciation of Milan – its church bells, its art and music – was soon eclipsed by a greater passion, and his debonair man-of-the-world pose evaporated when he realised he was in love again: timid, uncertain, vulnerable. He had been introduced to Angela Pietragrua in 1800, and dreamed of her on his return to Paris (she was 'dark-haired, superb, sexy...'). Here she was again, and he started claiming to himself that he had been, if not exactly faithful to her memory, at least constant for eleven years. His old shyness returned, and 'a terrible gloom filled my soul'. No matter how much he told himself that he expected little pleasure from possessing Angela (Angéline, all thighs and breasts, had put him off), he was still in thrall to her: no longer could he play the detached tourist; Milan was a battlefield, everything in it had meaning only insofar as it could serve or hinder his campaign to have her. All the pleasure he had derived from memories of his earlier visit to Milan evaporated. The idyll was over. Love, that 'illness', had him in its grip. He was even bored at La Scala; a visit to Leonardo's *Last Supper* left him cold; the great Biblioteca Ambrosiana failed to inspire this great bibliophile (mainly, it must be admitted, because of the chatter of all the *ciceroni*).

On 21st September 1811, '**at** half past eleven' in the morning, Angela yielded, but only after 'a grave moral struggle' in which HB acted out scenes of passion and despair. At half past one the following night, he left Milan for Bologna, Florence, Rome, Naples and Ancona, before another three weeks in Milan – all part of a detour back to Paris. Count Daru was furious at HB's unauthorised leave, and wrote to his wife, 'I thought Beyle had become a bit more reliable, but he's just acted in a really frivolous manner.' People were gossiping: maybe a singer was involved? This way, HB would never earn the promotion he craved. There was a difference between liking *opera buffa* and playing around with buffoons of women.

HB was thus now exploring Italy beyond Milan. He enjoyed travelling alone, or at least with only the locals for company. 'I need a certain dose of conversation and expansion [*épanchement*]; since I can't find this if I have a travelling companion, I get it from the Italians. In that way I'm forced to study them.' The echoes awoken in his soul by the mountains and the people among whom he was travelling would be spoiled by having to chatter to a witty Frenchman. Still, he grumbled to Pauline that the inns were often filthy, and ordinary people impatient and coarse.

In Florence it was pouring with rain, and the church interiors were even darker than usual. He made his way to Santa Croce, as a pilgrim to the tomb of the great Italian tragedian Alfieri. Inside, near Alfieri's tomb, were those of Michelangelo, Machiavelli, and Galileo. 'It has to be admitted that few churches are honoured by such tombs. It almost makes you want to be buried.' He was underwhelmed, however, by Michelangelo's tomb when he observed that the statues were held in place by crampons. Alfieri's was more imposing, but the figure of Italy weeping was a little graceless and plump, especially her fat thighs. Again he reflected bitterly on the way the French '**form of government**' made any great sculpture impossible. Machiavelli's tomb was spoiled by its pedantic inscriptions; Galileo's was dull... But the next minute he was standing in front of two pictures which gave him 'the strongest sensation' he had ever experienced from paintings. He was ravished, on the verge of tears; each detail made him drunk with pleasure. The paintings in question were the four sibyls by Baldassare Francesconi, known as *Il Volterrano* (1611–89). Hunkered down on the kneeler of a *prie-dieu*, his head thrown back, HB gazed up at them. Fifteen years later, in his *Rome, Naples and Florence*, he remembered his emotion; his judgement had not changed with time. 'Absorbed in the contemplation of sublime beauty, I saw it from close up, I could, so to speak, touch it.' He fell in love with one of the sibyls. Then the servant acting as his guide tugged his sleeve and showed him a painting of Christ's descent into Limbo. Even noting down the impression this painting made on him brought tears to his eyes. He even forgot how tired he was and the way his new boots were pinching his toes. He assumed that the 'Limbo' was by Guercino: he worshipped this painter in the depths of his heart. But a couple of hours later, he learned that it was in fact by Bronzino, a discovery that annoyed him, as did the insistence of other art-lovers present that its 'colouring' was 'weak'.

The other artistic riches of the city on the Arno brought on several attacks of 'Stendhal syndrome' or over-sensitivity to works of art.[47] He could also be cool in his appraisals. The figures of Christ were all soppy (*niais*). The bust of Brutus by Michelangelo had character and force, and HB admired it – but found the effect somewhat spoiled by the tendentious Latin inscription claiming that Michelangelo had left it unfinished when he suddenly remembered the tyrannicidal 'crime' of that great republican. In any case, Michelangelo had failed to capture the 'gentle soul' and 'poignant struggle depicted by Shakespeare' ('**In Julius Caesar**', as HB helpfully added in his diary). Surveying the inscriptions placed by husbands on the tombs of their wives, he at first smiled with affected contempt. But this was merely because he was wearing a '*frac français*'. When he forgot the need to sneer, when he became HB rather than just another superior, witty Frenchman, he was touched by the naturalness of these memorials, the inscriptions of which praised the wives for never causing quarrels and for treating their servants with kindness. He returned to see 'his' Volterrano Sibyl: her Germanic face reminded him of Minette, albeit very much 'noblified' (his neologism); a sweet expression, but with an eye that spoke of her grandiose soul. 'She is talking to God in a gentle, trusting way,' and she holds a marble tablet on which are written the words:

AQUAE
ELEVA
VERUNT
ARCAM[48]

But while he was admiring the 'Limbo' painting, a 'man of the people' came up to explain it to him. HB wished he would just bugger off, and stalked away from the painting. In his diary, he mused on the way his own judgements clashed with those of others. He had no proof his taste was any *better* than theirs. 'The only thing I can vouch for is that I write what I think. There are in Europe perhaps eight or ten people who think the same way as I do. I love those people even though I don't know them.' As for the rest, he despised them, and knew that they would probably feel the same way about him. He lived in this permanent state of antagonism towards a potential public that he also craved, if only for the sake of that group of people in it (never many in number) fortunate enough to grasp something of what he meant, and to have their natural melancholy assuaged thereby. He continued to watch and listen to the locals; the Florentines pronounced 'Carmine' – the name of a church – as 'Harmine', with a strongly aspirated 'h': perhaps this was a relic of ancient Roman pronunciation?

A trip to Naples was a little disappointing: everything seemed dead, the music was poor – and this time he found that travelling alone was less fun than if he had had a woman at his side to share impressions with (as, in Milan, he had Angela). He climbed Vesuvius and was taken aback to discover that there was no sight of hell bubbling away in the depths of its crater. The view from the hermit's hut up there was probably the most beautiful in the world. But yet another visitor's book filled with platitudes spoiled his visit (why did he always feel obliged to take a peek at these chronicles of tourist fatuousness?): he resigned himself to having been preceded by Mme de Staël, Schlegel, and Bigot de Préameneu, State Councillor of France. It was early October;

the grapes were still on the vine – but the local wine, *lacrima Christi*, he found 'undrinkable'. In Isola Bella, he read Ossian as the rain fell and the thunder rumbled. He started to receive worryingly cold letters from Angela. All autumn he suffered from insomnia, kept awake by coffee, travel, and sensations; he lost weight, but felt well. 'I repeat: I am enjoying the best of health.' (Why would he 'repeat' such an observation in a private diary?)

Reunited with Angela, he spent an hour and a half with her. **'She seemed to have pleasure. For my own acount** [sic] **I made that two times, and for her three or four**,' then went out to the Brera and surveyed with satisfaction paintings by Giotto and Mantegna. He thought with renewed zest of his latest idea: writing a history of Italian painting.

Russia

O Rus'!
Pushkin

If I succeed in Russia, I will be master of the world.
Napoleon

On 16th March 1812, one evening at the Duke of Cadore's house in Paris, HB mused over an attractive, big-breasted woman: her eyes were lovely *and yet stupid*. He spent some time musing over this anomaly in his diary, illustrating it with five detailed sketches of various curves of eyelid: the last of these resembles a geometrician's study of ellipses intersected by a straight line. He was bringing his mathematical skills to bear on the tiniest details of his 'sensations'.

War with Russia became inevitable; HB was ordered to make his way to the river Dvina. Having been granted an audience with the Empress of France (she conversed about his route, the difficulties of the journey, etc.) he went to pay his respects to the infant King of Rome (who was fast asleep), and left Paris in the early hours of 23rd July. He viewed the forthcoming campaign as one big hunting expedition. He passed through Weimar and joined his regiment on 14th August 1812: he was now part of the vastest military operation that the world had yet seen. Smolensk went up in flames; Napoleon was exhilarated at the sight, comparing it to 'an eruption of Vesuvius'. The expedition proved to be an exhausting affair and one evening, at dinner, the guests around HB all went to sleep with their forks still in their hands. He wrote to his friend Félix Faure that he was living in 'an ocean of barbarity', feeling entirely unambitious, and cheered only by a little music played on an out-of-tune piano by an incompetent musician. In his letters to Félix, HB started to set out the principles of *Beylism*, which was largely the converse of *Rousseauism*: Jean-Jacques had seen virtues and duties everywhere, and had never overcome his propensity to pedantry – hence his unhappiness. Jean-Jacques was clearly not one of the *Beylist* elect (of whom there are never very many).

On 28th August, sixty leagues away from Moscow, he found himself sitting at the foot of a dead birch-tree, in a dust-filled little wood. He was irritated by the absence of water and books, by the filthy ground with its dead leaves, its dry branches and its ants, and by the lack of a clean change of clothes. He felt that he was surrounded by idiots. 'I feel totally fed-up. I don't write a diary when I'm happy [as we have seen, this is not true]; indiscreet analysis of that kind ruins my happiness, but today I've got nothing to lose. I've been cold since nine o'clock.'

Napoleon, arms folded, surveyed the 'Asiatic capital' from the Poklonny Hill as his men threw their caps into the dusty air and shouted '*Moscou! Moscou!*' Only a small fraction now remained of the greatest army ever assembled: thousands of them had already perished of hunger and disease. General Kutuzov, that embodiment of the cunning and obstinacy of the Russian people, had retreated. Moscow, the Third Rome of the prophecies, was abandoned;[49] the number of crows in the Kremlin had increased, just as it had in the early seventeenth-century Time of Troubles with its royal pretenders and its anarchy.[50] It was an ill omen. On 14th September, the French duly entered the strangely quiet city, looking about the empty streets suspiciously. Baron Claude François de Méneval described the scene in these words: 'No noise disturbed the solitude of the city streets, except for the rumble of the cannon and the ammunition wagons. Moscow appeared to be in a deep sleep, like the enchanted cities we read about in Arabian tales.' By and large, only the lower classes and a few merchants and dealers had remained.[51] Napoleon made his way straight to the Kremlin; here, amid the tombs of the tsars, he paced up and down, stopping occasionally to glare at the brooding eyes of Christ Pantocrator. Why would Alexander not admit he was beaten? Where were the emissaries offering bread and salt, and all the traditional tokens of surrender?

HB, too, was a little frustrated in Moscow, mainly because of the absence of decent music: he had imagined yet more nights at the opera, and a populace that would, like the Italians – or at least some of them – greet Napoleon as a liberator. Soon after Napoleon's entry into the Kremlin, fires started to break out in the so-called 'Chinese town' (*Kitaigorod*); this had been ablaze for some hours when HB, talking to M. Daru in the courtyard of the Apraxine Palace, noticed flames flickering close to them. They hurried to control the fire. Although it was only September, the cold was intense and had given HB toothache. A soldier had just been spotted jabbing his bayonet into a man carrying a barrel of beer; HB drew his sword and would have run the villain through, but the malefactor was simply taken to the Governor's, who released him. HB and Daru (in an even worse mood than usual, shouting orders and swearing at his men) returned to the palace, where they tried to get a fire-pump going. HB, still tormented by toothache, slept fitfully until 7 a.m., when he loaded his carriage and joined the queue of the departing French: it had been decided to move away from the fires, which were now approaching rapidly. The carriages remained blocked on the boulevard for five or six hours; impatient at the delay, HB went off to take a closer look at the conflagration. He stopped off at a house where a colleague was billeted, and with some of his fellow soldiers drank three bottles of wine 'which restored life to us'.

His spirits were also improved by reading a few lines of an English translation of *Virginie*.[52] Outside, in the general chaos of the smoke-filled streets, soldiers were lashing out with their sabres. Many of them helped themselves to as much booty as they could carry: some even darted into the flames, where they risked being roasted alive. When HB returned to his waiting carriage, he told his servants to fill it up with the flour and oats that had been discovered in a local storehouse. They were slow to obey, and he was again shocked at the lack-adaisical discipline of the French. This was the kind of thing that tried his patience and made him lose his temper. Unlike his colleagues, he could not simply shake off impertinent and insulting remarks: he was just too sensitive. He made his way back to the Kremlin; the French were desperately trying to work out how to stop the fire from spreading, but Count Rostopchin, the Russian Military Governor of Moscow, had been an efficient fire-raiser.

The flames were now roaring high up into the sky and turning the atmosphere a copper colour. The stench of burning was everywhere: the sight was 'horrible' and 'weird', according to French General de Fezensac. HB's manservant (like so many others) was completely drunk and busied himself with pillaging as much as he could and piling it into HB's carriage: tablecloths, wine, a violin for his own use… Eventually, there was hardly enough room for HB himself, and he was forced to walk alongside it while his 'bloody coward' (*foireux*) of a servant managed the restless horses. Before leaving, HB, forever short of reading matter, pillaged a volume by Voltaire, the one called *Facéties*, bound in red morocco. (Though he was convinced that Russia was essentially a poor country, with scrubby, monotonous landscapes, he was pleasantly surprised, even on the retreat, by the splendour of the big Russian town mansions, almost all of which seemed to contain the complete works of Voltaire.) His colleagues criticised him for breaking up such a fine set of books. The house was, admittedly, on fire – but surely HB could have tried to keep all the volumes together? HB himself later admitted to some remorse over his vandalism.

When the carriages set off, they initially had to head straight towards the flames. The smoke made it difficult to breathe; the drivers were eventually forced to turn round, their pillage-laden carriages cumbersomely manoeuvring. The 'absolute lack of any order or prudence' increased their danger, thought HB. To his pleasure, General Kirgener bellowed at the drunken, sleepy servants that they'd better show some bloody initiative if they were going to get out of this mess alive. In the rout, HB's column of carriages collided with that of the King of Naples, Murat, who had been providing sterling service to Napoleon (HB thought Murat was a brave soldier, a bit of an actor with his two-foot-high plumes waving over his hat, but possessed of an invaluable 'gaiety'). There was bickering over who had right of way; coach drivers lashed out with their whips, red-faced moustachioed men glared at each other; but HB's carriage was soon rumbling down the Tver road. 'We emerged from the city, illuminated as it was by the most beautiful blaze in the world, forming an immense pyramid that was like the prayers of the faithful, with its base resting on the earth and its pinnacle in the heavens.' The fire had been stoked by sofas and pianos, and a sinister moon hovered over the red flames and black smoke.

HB's carriage headed towards the Petrovski Palace, northwest of Moscow, where Napoleon was to stay. All of a sudden, HB saw Daru's calash topple over into a ditch ahead of him; it was righted only with considerable difficulty. Daru, inevitably, roared with anger and frustration. A few years later HB (who, for all his peevishness, kept a cool head in a crisis) could still remember how 'petty' his superior had seemed just then. As for Napoleon, HB later told Byron that the Emperor had started acting like a madman, signing orders with the name 'Pompey'; on the retreat he was morose and walked amid his soldiers clutching a white baton, since his horse kept slipping on the ice. Grizzled grenadiers pointed accusing fingers at him: 'That's the man who's got us all killed!' The Emperor looked at them; they burst into tears.

Finally, once he had settled down in his bivouac, HB had supper: raw fish, figs, and wine. He was already feeling hungover from the plonk he had pillaged. This had been 'one of the most annoying, and boringly annoying, days in my life'. He sent his journal pages detailing the evacuation of Moscow to Pauline, for her to send on to his friend Félix Faure, since he wanted to preserve some record of these 'insipid sufferings'. It appears, inevitably, that he made up many of his anecdotes about the Russian campaign. He himself traded on the idea that he had never really been there: no, that was his brother, Henri-Marc; HB, or so he claimed, had simply stolen the latter's papers – they had the same initials.[53] But he had, in spite of his teasing, really witnessed 'that grand experiment upon the heart of man', that 'deplorable catastrophe' as he later described the retreat for the benefit of an English newspaper. Our Chinaman[54] had lived through interesting times.

He was now appointed Director General of Reserve Supplies for a wide area including Smolensk, a job he undertook with brisk efficiency, aware that the army would march better on stomachs that had something inside them. He wondered whether he would survive; he wrote to Pauline, 'Farewell; write to me and remember to enjoy yourself; life is brief.'

Decline and fall

A king is the slave of history.

Tolstoy

The *Grande Armée* staggered back to Europe, harassed by starvation, thirst, disease, winter, peasants, and Cossacks. Many French soldiers were left in the snows of Russia, including HB's cousin Gaéton Gagnon. A trip to Russia was well worthwhile, HB wrote sardonically to Félix Faure on 7th November 1812: you were attacked by Cossacks and often spent the night thinking that the next day would mean death or capture. As the noise of the cannon drew nearer in the night time, the French were forced back on their own courage, 'face to face with destiny'. Curiously, years later, he was reminded of this by the Sistine Chapel ceiling, and 'the figure of the eternal Being creating the first man out of a void'. The Cossacks pillaged his supplies, and for eighteen days he lived on ration bread and water. Every evening the French had to build a primitive shelter out of dry wood. His fingers froze; the letters he sent were in even more illegible handwriting than usual. The soldiers moved forward with caution, halting frequently enough for HB to get through almost a whole volume of the letters of Madame du Deffand, the French literary hostess and correspondent of Voltaire. HB later told Mérimée that he couldn't remember how he had eaten, apart from a piece of mutton fat that he bought for twenty francs. On the third day of the retreat from Moscow, HB and some 1,500 men had found themselves separated from the rest of the French Army by a considerable detachment of Russians. His fellow soldiers spent the night moaning that they would all be killed. Then some other soldiers, made of sterner stuff, harangued them in fine military style: 'You load of bloody riffraff! You're all going to fucking die tomorrow, you're too fucking incompetent to handle a rifle!' etc. As dawn broke, the duly encouraged French advanced resolutely through the mist towards the fires of the Russian bivouac. They found a solitary dog. The Russians had decamped during the night.

Near the river Berezina, HB, freshly shaved and dressed with some care, presented himself to Pierre Daru. 'You've had a shave!' said Daru. 'That's the spirit!' Another *auditeur*, M. Bergonié, later claimed he owed his life to HB; the latter, suspecting that the bridges over the Berezina were likely to be overburdened by the crush of French attempting to get across, persuaded Bergonié to cross over just in time. HB's premonitions were proved correct: the crossing of the Berezina on 26th–29th November cost some 20,000 French lives. Napoleon's soldiers either drowned in the freezing waters of the river or were trampled underfoot by their stampeding comrades. Another 10,000 were cut down by Cossacks.

HB now realised how disastrous Napoleon's Russian gamble had proved. But HB's own sojourn in Moscow had not been entirely wasted: it had given him time to think. He now realised that he liked *opera buffa* so much because it provided him with 'the sensation of the ideal perfection of comedy'. Amid scenes of apocalyptic devastation, freezing cold, hungry, exhausted, he clung to the idea of a human comedy, preferably set to music.

HB's journey back home went: Moscow (which he left on 16th October 1812), Smolensk, Vilna (the remnants of the *Grande Armée* that managed to get this far had been reduced to a starving band of desperadoes), and Königsberg, where he spent Christmas and heard Mozart's opera about a beneficent dictator menaced by fire-raisers and conspirators, *La Clemenza di Tito*. Then Danzig, Stargard, Berlin (he left the city on the day he turned thirty), Brunswick, Kassel, Frankfurt (where he managed to catch up on some sleep), the Rhine, and Paris, where he arrived on 31st January. In Danzig, he started a new diary (and headed it 'Chapter 1', suggesting an oddly 'public' presentation of his intimate thoughts), having lost, on the Russian campaign, not only his Brunswick diary for 1806 and 1807, but twelve out of thirteen volumes of his projected *History of Painting in Italy*, as well as the notes he had made on a volume of Chesterfield, pillaged (like the Voltaire) during the retreat from Moscow. He quailed at the idea of having to reread all the stuff he had combed for his *History* (but in any case, right now he felt *dead*, more frigid in spirit than a man of sixty). As for his diaries, he tried to console himself with the thought that, if anybody else found them, they would probably not be able to make head nor tail of them, since neither could he. 'I have no memory, none whatsoever, so when I am discreet in the diaries **of my life** that I've kept up until now, after a year or two I can't understand a single thing.'

In Paris, to try and rekindle spirits that had been frozen by the snows of Russia, he plunged back into the study of 'the comic' and of philosophy (Helvétius), and re-embarked on his never-ending *Letellier*. His only real pleasures now lay in reminiscence; he was even wary of going to see the pictures in the Musée Napoléon as their presence would merely remind him cruelly of his current apathy. As an *auditeur*, he kept his ears pricked for news of promotion. The Emperor would surely find some fitting reward for a man who had shown such sangfroid and capability in the Russian campaign? So he felt justified in dreaming of a prefecture in one of the fourteen *départements* of occupied Italy…

Some of his old zest for life rekindled when he was given a copy of the speech (currently circulating in *samizdat*) that Chateaubriand had prepared to deliver at his reception into the French Academy. The original text had provoked Napoleon's displeasure; Chateaubriand refused to change it; he was not received into the Academy. HB read it in the Café de Foy, and found it mediocre and false. He thought Chateaubriand lacked *tone*, and talked about himself too much; his comments on Milton were palpably wrongheaded; he was far from the 'great good taste of Antiquity'. And HB concluded, 'This man **shall not outlive his century**': in 1913, nobody would read him. HB made fun of another 'Ichmicher' (a name he made up from two German words meaning an 'I-me-er'), possibly Pierre Daru, and he later found Chateaubriand's account of his travels to Jerusalem 'stank of egotism and egoism'. Curiously, it is HB who popularised two words that have come to stand for so many of the pleasures and pains of the modern subject, 'tourist' and 'egotist'. There must have been a difference between HB's egotism (as in his *Memoirs of an Egotist*) and that of Chateaubriand: perhaps in HB's view the difference resided mainly in the degree of self-consciousness: *he* was egotistic and knew it ('What is real for each person if not his or her own existence?' he wrote; and 'Everything worthwhile in this world is oneself'), while Chateaubriand was just fatuously self-important even when he thought he was being objective.

For the first few months of 1813, HB was worried that he might be sent back to join the Army. He was indeed duly commanded to reassume his duties as *auditeur* in Germany – and thus witnessed the only 'classical' battle he ever saw: the one fought at Bautzen in May 1813. Or rather, he did not witness it; he was there, but the smoke, the confusion and the pouring rain made it impossible to catch more than chaotic glimpses of this indecisive encounter. He did, however, hear the constant roar of the cannon, booming through the thick murk.

In summer 1813 HB was in Erfurt, and then in Sagan in Silesia, managing the hospital and reading Tacitus; here he succumbed to one of the fevers going round. The epidemic was severe, and the fever could be fatal, but he wrote to Pauline to say that the 'closeness of death' had little effect on him. He convalesced, slowly, in Dresden. Even the *Matrimonio segreto* failed to cure him; he emerged from the performance feeling more ill than ever.

In September 1813 he was back in Milan. He had just bought a new pair of trousers in grey kerseymere; sitting in the Café Nuovo, he lifted a cup of coffee *alla panera* to his lips (in his diary he used the Milanese term *panera* for *panna*, or cream). His hand trembled, either from emotion at being back in Milan or from the remnant of the fever contracted in Sagan; he spilled the coffee on his new trousers. Now that he was back in Italy, he felt more original, more 'himself', but the rapture was less than on his first visits. On an excursion to Monza he remembered, on 21st September 1813, that this was the anniversary of Angela's surrender: he had noted the date and the time (11.30 a.m.) on the braces that he had presumably taken off to accomplish his amorous victory, and the details were still visible there. He was hoping for a job in Rome or Florence. He resumed his liaison with Angela, who, pleading her anxiety at the danger of being discovered, resorted to a complex semiology: the position of her windows (open, half-open, shut, draped or not) would tell him at what time she would be free. She rarely was.

HB was ordered back to take charge of the defence of the Dauphiné against the invading Allies.

On 12th January 1814, he wrote to the Duc de Feltre, 'It appears that the enemy is receiving reinforcements in Geneva. Morale in Savoy is bad; we have only 1,780 men to defend all the places in the Hautes-Alpes and Dauphiné!' HB, under the command of the Count de Saint-Vallier, insisted that the French soldiers be well fed and properly paid: otherwise, it would be so easy for them to slink away into the mountains. Although poorly (he was still suffering from the after-effects of his Silesian fever), he was active in organising supplies of munitions (guns were in short supply). He decided it would be necessary to force the Bishop of Grenoble to publish a directive ordering his priests (whom HB suspected of being in league with the invading Allies) to rally to the defence of their 'prince' (Napoleon) and their *'patrie'*. But this did not stop a *Te Deum* from being sung in the cathedral of Chambéry when the Mont-Blanc was occupied by the enemy.[55] HB rejoiced – at least in his official letters – at the soldierly zeal of the Dauphiné. 'The sound of cannon fire sanctifies all measures,' and French soldiers could be bivouacked on the local inhabitants – who would naturally rush out of their houses to offer wine and lodgings at the sight of a blue uniform. But soon, in Les Échelles (where, as we have seen, HB had spent some of his happiest days as a child at the home of his uncle Romain Gagnon), French conscripts were throwing down their weapons and fleeing or surrendering. The fall of Geneva became increasingly probable; HB started to think about making his way back to Paris, if he could slip through the hordes of Cossacks charging across central France. The Cossacks filled the French with dread; they were said to be very cruel, especially towards women – 'So they should be,' said HB, flippantly, though he had reason to remember with a shudder the savagery of the retreat from Moscow. In a letter to Pauline, he described the current state of affairs as a tragedy worthy of Shakespeare, especially as the once mighty Murat, King of Naples was allegedly going mad, and succumbing to fits of weeping as he hurried impotently from Bologna to Ferrara and back again. By mid-March, HB was in Lyon and then, finally, in Paris, where he observed the Battles of Pantin and Montmartre. Both fell to the enemy.

The Empress and the Court quitted Paris on 29th March and the Allies entered two days later; to general surprise, they neither burned the city down nor indulged in more than moderate pillaging. The Cossacks contented themselves with asking the waiters in the cafés on the Champs-Élysées to get a move on: *'Bistro! Bistro!'* ('Quick! Quick!') they would shout – a word that still makes the *garçons* jump. HB himself, despite his chilly memories of the Moscow campaign, fell momentarily for the charms of a Russian aide-de-camp sitting next to him at a performance of Beaumarchais's *The Barber of Seville* one evening in May. He sensed the first stirrings of love, felt bashful, and found the young man so alluring that he did not dare look at him for long.

Such encounters brightened the gloom only temporarily. HB had no job (and little chance of getting one if the Bourbons were restored; he had backed the wrong man – Napoleon had abdicated unconditionally on 6th April), no income, and 37,000 francs' worth of debts. He even had to sell his horses. Caught up in the debate of what shape a post-Napoleonic Europe should assume, he and two friends (Louis de Bellisle – whom he nicknamed 'Fairisland' – and Louis Crozet) discussed a new constitution for France. He wrote, for instance, in 'Thoughts on the Constitution': 'I fervently hope that every time I use the word *liberty*, the reader will not think I mean that chimerical liberty which is made for angels alone, the liberty that several passionate souls dreamed of in 1789 and which was drowned in floods of the purest blood. *My* liberty is inseparable from a nobility and a king.' Louis XVIII could perhaps be counted on to establish a constitutional monarchy that would safeguard some of the liberties acquired by the 'eternal principles' of the French Revolution: HB concluded a manifesto-letter of 1st May 1814 by claiming that the cries of 'Vive le roi!' and 'Vive la liberté!' belonged together. – But, the following day, he was already back-pedalling: a constitution would make everyone 'serious', the French would lose their 'natural gaiety' and become as pompous about being 'free under the law' as the English. A couple of days later he was again singing the praises of a constitution, which would at least limit the powers of the monarchy... But then it was HB's own constitution that started to preoccupy him: he was suffering from pneumonia after running around Paris like a headless chicken, trying to work out how to pay off his debts and resisting, barely, the temptation to blow his brains out.

He continued to brood over politics; he drew up plans for a new 'electoral law' and for a College of Peers to repair the damage done to education by Napoleon, who had made the fatal error of suppressing the Écoles centrales: 'There was nothing in this world the Emperor Napoleon feared so much as public education,' HB later wrote in his *Life of Rossini*. Its syllabus would consist of arithmetic and algebra, geometry and probability, the *Idéologie* of Destutt de Tracy, the history and constitution of England with particular attention to the period from 1600 onwards, the history of France from 1715–1814, and a general study of modern constitutions and existing governments. Article XXXII ran: 'Every day during dinner, a student will read aloud the official articles of the *Journal Officiel*.' This was a government organ packed with useful information.

As a man identified closely with the now-fallen imperial regime, HB came under suspicion and, indeed, police surveillance. A report on 'M. de Beyle' dated Paris, 31st March 1814, reads as follows:

He is a plump fellow, born in Grenoble, aged thirty-one, living at no. 3 rue Neuve-du-Luxembourg. His acquaintances are MM. Crozet, Faure, De Bellisle, de Barrel, de Mareste, de Courtivron, Mure.

He very rarely goes to salons. The houses he frequents are those of Mme Daru, Mme de Pallavicini, MMmes de Baure and Lebrun, his relatives, and Mme de Longueville.

He goes to the theatre frequently and is always living with some actress. When not engaged on official activity, he works four or five hours a day on making historical extracts and notes on his travels. His copyist is a rather bad sort, Fougeol by name.

For a long time he lived with an actress from the Opéra Buffa, but it appears they have split up. He never misses a performance at the Opéra Buffa. He spends his evenings there, or else at the [Théâtre] Français.

He always lunches at the café de Foy and dines at the Frères Provençaux.[56] He buys a great number of books. He returns home every evening at midnight.

This police report – a *brief life* of HB – is in HB's own hand-writing. Perhaps he had been spying on himself?

On 26th December 1814, he observed the full moon through a Herschel telescope.

He would frequently turn up at the home of the Countess Beugnot in the requisite silk stockings, hoping that her husband's support would be of use in finding an official position. He flirted with her, too, but any *tendresse* between the Countess and her silk-stockinged suitor seems to have evaporated: when he dedicated his *Lives of Haydn etc.* to her, under the name 'Madame d'Oligny', he referred to the 'cloud' that had overshadowed their relationship. Ten years later, he took her daughter the Countess Clémentine Curial as his lover.

Feeling increasingly alienated from events, he hired a copyist and, in his own words, 'dictated a corrected translation of the lives of Haydn, Mozart and Metastasio, based on an Italian work'.

Seeking Haydn

With sudden leap the flexible tiger appears.

Anonymous English librettist of Haydn's The Creation

In *The Life of Henry Brulard*, HB later wrote, 'Music has perhaps been my strongest and most costly passion: it still endures now that I am fifty-two and is more intense than ever. I would walk I don't know how many leagues, or put up with I don't know how many days in prison, to hear *Don Giovanni* and the *Matrimonio segreto*, and I don't know if there's anything else for which I would make such an effort!' He projected his love of music onto his heroes – Napoleon, for instance. 'He often smiled, but never laughed,' HB remarked of the Emperor. 'I saw him really enjoying himself on only one occasion; this was when he heard Crescentini singing the aria *Ombra adorata aspetta*.'[57]

HB now turned to music as a source of income. He based his biography of Haydn closely – very closely – on *Le Haydine, ovvero Lettere sulla vita e le opere del celebre maestro Giuseppe Haydn*, published in Milan in the year 1812 by the Italian librettist Giuseppe Carpani who had translated the words of Haydn's *Creation* into Italian. Carpani had met Haydn in Vienna. HB had not – though he had, as we saw, attended Haydn's funeral, which was the next best thing. HB set to work translating, paraphrasing, cutting, and pasting. He added a life of Mozart, explicitly stating that he had translated it from a German work by Friedrich von Schlichtegroll (who also wrote 'An Essay on the Triple Inscription Found at Rosetta in Egypt'), while in fact mainly drawing on a short work by Théophile Frédéric Winckler (1771–1807) published in Paris in 1801. (This latter work itself derived much of its material from Schlichtegroll.) HB added a few stories from *Thirty-two Anecdotes on W.C. Mozart*, translated from Rochlitz by C.F. Cramer. When it came to Metastasio, HB relied heavily on an Italian critic by the name of Giuseppe Baretti, a friend of Dr Johnson. HB always remained close to his sources, and sometimes embraced them with the deadly zeal of a python strangling its prey.

Thus was born the work that HB described, in his dedication, as 'the first I have ever written'. But it was not by HB, or even Henri (de) Beyle, but signed by a certain Louis-Alexandre-César Bombet, a name of hilariously imperial bombast (HB himself later referred to his *opus bombeticum*). Louis XVIII, Tsar Alexander I... Did he wish to mock the new Europe by implying that its rulers were plagiarists and thieves like himself?

30th June, in his *Journal*: 'I've been working since 10th May on Metastasio and Mozart. Anyway, this work gives me a great deal of pleasure, and takes away the pain of M.D. [M. Doligny, his code name for Beugnot] not appointing me as a secretary to the Florence Embassy.' By the time it was printed, he had left Paris (perhaps piqued at his failure to seduce the Countess Beugnot), and so could not correct the proofs: the published work, riddled with errors, some of them due to poor proofreading and some due to his own mistakes,[58] had a first print run of a thousand. After ten years it had still not shifted more than 127 copies. This was a terrible blow to HB, who had been hoping for a modest best-seller on whose royalties he would be able to afford a three-month trip to Philadelphia. It was soon translated into English (496 pages: Murray, 1817) by Gardiner, author of the 'Sacred Melodies', whose version was praised by HB (though it introduced a few extra mistakes of its own). HB claims to have been strolling down 'Almarle-Street' in London when he spotted this translation of 'his' work in the shop window of the publisher John Murray: he was impressed by the new notes provided by 'G.' (Gardiner) and wondered briefly about translating them into French for his own next edition, before deciding that he didn't want his work to seem 'too pedantic'.

The author of the *Haydine* which HB had so insouciantly appropriated, Carpani, became aware of the book by 'Bombet' in the middle of 1815. He sent off two wittily angry letters to *Le Constitutionnel*. It was not just HB's blatant plagiarism of his remarks on Haydn that annoyed him: it was the almost mocking way in which the French writer had stolen some of his most personal anecdotes. Carpani had suffered from a fever in Vienna, and been cured by listening to a Haydn Mass, as one might expect, on St Anne's Day, 26th July, 1799.[59] And exactly the same thing had happened to Bombet! How curious! Bombet had pinched his fever – and also stolen his medicine!

Carpani produced an affidavit by five members of the Viennese public, including that fine composer and collaborator of Mozart, Antonio Salieri, First Kappelmeister of the Imperial and Royal Court of Vienna and author of the splendid opera *Prima la musica e poi le parole* ('Music First and Words Afterwards'). They swore that they had never come across this Bombet (contrary to his claims), and thus could not have told him anything at all about Haydn. In May 1816, *Le Constitutionnel* published a reply, by (or inspired by) HB, claiming simultaneously – and a little contradictorily – 1) that it was Bombet's work that had been plagiarised by Carpani and 2) that, in any case, if the work *had* been originally in Italian it deserved to be translated into French (and if it were French, into Italian). 'M. Bombet's book, original or copy, is on sale in Paris chez M. Didot, rue du Pont-de-Lodi.' Carpani replied that if this was a joke, it was in bad taste. Whereupon Bombet's younger brother, 'H.C.G. Bombet' (HB, of course) waded into the fray, with a poignant and indignant letter that began: 'M. Louis-Alexandre-César Bombet, my brother, is in London; he is a very old man, suffering from gout, bothering his head hardly at all with music and even less with M. Carpani...' This obsession with plagiarism was ridiculous! Did Hume *plagiarise* Rapin-Thoiras when he claimed that Elizabeth I was the daughter of Henry VIII? Carpani found himself challenged to publish thirty pages of Bombet's work together with thirty pages of Carpani simply translated into French, and allow the public to judge which was the better work.

Carpani did some detective work and eventually concluded that 'Bombet' was merely a pseudonym for the same man who had published *The History of Painting in Italy* under the pseudonym Aubertin: behind these two *noms de plume* was a certain 'E.B.' (for Enrico Beyle) from Grenoble.

Carpani died in 1825: the controversy fizzled out. In 1841, Quérard published his great work on *Literary Hoaxes Unveiled*: apparently, HB told him that he had reluctantly suppressed his original desire to state clearly that the work by 'Bombet' had been imitated from the Italian. His publisher had told him to avoid all mention of an original, astutely pointing out that translations never sell.

On a close reading, the *Life of Haydn* betrays HB/Bombet's love of playing the game while (almost) giving it away. In letter XXII (the work is cast in an epistolary form) he says quite explicitly, 'There is perhaps not a single sentence in this little book that has not been translated from some foreign work.' In a letter to his friend Mareste, in April 1820, he claimed that when Molière said 'I pick up my material from wherever I find it' [*je prends mon bien où je le trouve*], Molière was himself copying Cyrano de Bergerac.

The *Life of Haydn* is an oddly characteristic first work for HB to have published, fleshing out anecdote with imagination. Bombet claims to have visited the ageing composer in 1808, when Haydn was a decrepit, melancholy figure, sunk in apathy, but still able to regale Bombet with his memories. 'Haydn told me...' that from his youth onwards he had worked sixteen and sometimes eighteen hours a day; he had given Bombet a glass of Tokay, and gently corrected his opinions on Handel, Mozart et al. The book compares and contrasts music and the visual arts (especially Raphael, Correggio, and Leonardo). Bombet dwells on music's not being a pictorial art and ponders on the possibility of uniting the arts of hearing and sight:

> I have often thought that the effect of the symphonies of Haydn and Mozart would be greatly increased if they were played in the orchestra pit of a theatre while excellent *décorations* analogous to the main ideas in the different pieces succeeded each other on stage. A fine *décoration* representing a calm sea and a vast and pure sky would, it seems to me, increase the effect of an *andante* by Haydn depicting happiness and tranquillity.

Letter XIII includes a very lengthy footnote (with footnotes to the footnote) plugging the virtues of Cimarosa, just in case there were those who had not heard his music. Letter XIV includes the 'translation' of a notice on the music of Naples, with a helpful list of the dates of twenty composers (many of the details are incorrect), only some of whom spent any significant time in Naples. Towards the end of Letter XVI we learn that, when Haydn depicts the emotions of a penitent sinner, he sometimes uses triple time (the tempo of the waltz or the *contredanse*), which unfortunately has the effect of making the sins seem too tempting.[60] HB then shoulders Carpani and even Bombet aside to proselytise for one of his own favourite *philosophes* and provide us with a suitably physiological semiotics of music: 'Cabanis will tell you that joy accelerates the movement of the blood, and requires a *presto*; sadness is lowering, slows the flow of the humours, and brings us to a *tempo largo*; contentment requires the major mode; melancholy is expressed by the minor mode: this last truth is the foundation of the styles of Cimarosa and Mozart.' The final essay is on the state of music in Italy. An audience listening to a piece by Piccini will easily recognise the tunes that he has pinched from Sacchini,[61] whereupon they start shouting, 'Bravo, Sacchini!'

The History of Painting: an Italian chronicle

> Rough sketches dashed off in the heat of inspiration
> express the artist's ideas in a few quick strokes, while
> too much diligent hard work sometimes saps the vitality
> and abilities of those who never know when to leave off.
> *Vasari*

Unwilling to hang around in France under a regime that might simply dispense with his services forthwith, HB now decided to return to Italy: by August he was back in Milan, embroiled with Angela Pietragrua (or 'Countess Simonetta', as he called her). She told him that her husband was terribly jealous, and forced HB to stay in Turin (where, in any case, he had spotted a 'philosophical' *chanteuse* with the loveliest eyes in the world) and to visit her, incognito, every ten days; on these occasions he was obliged to stay in a shabby inn. He even had to pay the chambermaid to let him in from the cold street. But the chambermaid, feeling ashamed at taking part in such deception, felt obliged to reveal to him that Angela was entertaining other lovers during HB's absences in Turin. To test her claim, he hid in a *cabinet* and spied through the keyhole as Angela and her current *beau* enjoyed each other's company. At first, the sheer ridiculousness of the situation filled HB with mirth, and he had to stifle his laughter; only later did unhappiness overwhelm him. Angela pleaded for forgiveness; he at first (depressed, betrayed, too proud to relent) withheld it; eventually, he started to take a certain 'physical pleasure' in encouraging her to detail all of her infidelities.[62]

On an excursion to Florence in October – the river Arno had almost dried up, the weather was chilly and he was eating in greasy spoons to save money: never had he felt more sensitive to the fine arts – he pursued his idea of writing a history of painting in Italy, convinced that he could avoid the insipid 'monarchical style' of most catalogues, whose only way of criticising a painter was to omit any praise. Thinking of the need to vary his style a little, he tried out several ways of stating that a certain painting is located in Pisa:

'I saw in Pisa…'

'You can see in Pisa, at the house of M. Montecatini…'

'You can see in Pisa…'

'He did a portrait that can be found in Pisa…'

'The traveller must not neglect…'

'The curious can see in Pisa…'

'To leave Pisa without seeing the painting, etc., would be a…'

Etc.

He struggled to express his feelings within the academic format of a history of painting: for one thing, the more enthusiastic he was, the more frigid his style. He wondered whether Diderot might be correct: it is better to mimic passion at a distance, rather than trying to convey it directly. But he *must* make the effort: who else was there to teach the French about real art, of which they were 'totally ignorant'?

He quarrelled, again, with Angela over the Christmas and New Year period 1814–15 (he had already decided in October that 'Love has been killed off'; on 22nd December she threatened him with the police). In January 1815 he heard from Pierre Daru that his wife, whom HB had loved, was dead.

He was still unsure (as Napoleon escaped from Elba and marched towards Paris) where in Italy to live. Naples? It was 'peopled by demons' – probably a political, not a theological observation. The city was now occupied by Ferdinand IV of Bourbon: the King of Naples, Murat, whom HB had seen during the great traffic-jam in Moscow, fled to Corsica but was later captured and shot on Ferdinand's orders. In any case, HB soon learned that he would not be appointed to the Consulate in Naples. Rome? But in Rome you had to be too hypocritical if you were to survive. Florence and Genoa were dull, Padua too small. It had to be either Venice or Milan.

At half past two on 19th July, in the café Florian, Venice,[63] he read of the capitulation of Paris: Napoleon had been vanquished in his last battle, near a small town in Belgium. 'All is lost,' wrote HB in his diary, 'even honour.' He would later say, in the kind of grandiose comparison that he detested in Chateaubriand, that he had risen and fallen with Napoleon: but his diary for the days after Waterloo is filled with notes on society dinners, on a pretty little garden he had spotted, on his reading (even good Italian prose tends to indulge in commonplaces, he notes), and on a new idea for 'a didactic poem' to explain the constitution of Great Britain to the peoples of the world.

Meanwhile he took instantly to the gaiety of Venice. Women were allowed much more freely into cafés than elsewhere, and social life went on until 2 a.m. It was so easy to pick up a woman! You sit next to her, and join (quite unselfconsciously) in the conversation. Repeat the procedure on subsequent occasions: within a fortnight, if the feelings are mutual, you are riding in a gondola with her, your hands wandering freely about her person. 'My happiness consists in being solitary in the middle of a big city,' he wrote. He had written similar things before. Now he added, 'And spending every night with a mistress. Venice fulfils these conditions perfectly.' Even the relative absence of trees along the *rii* was no drawback.

Those bastards the legitimists, meanwhile, were conniving in

Paris. It would have been better for France if the whole Bourbon family had become extinct. In October 1815, HB decided that trying to write about political events in France was useless: things were moving too fast. He wrote a draft of a dedication to *The History of Painting in Italy*, to 'His Majesty Napoleon the Great, Emperor, detained on the Isle of St Helena'. This dedication is yet another clue to the work's real subject: like so many of HB's works, it is a coded, indirect, but radical analysis of the political mire of post-Napoleonic Europe (in his laconic words 'After glory, mud').[64] Speaking truth to (fallen) power, HB's projected preface rebuked Napoleon for his 'detestable system of education' which had left France without strong and independent leaders apart from the Emperor himself; and Napoleon had lost heart too easily after Waterloo, instead of making himself dictator of France. Still, he had founded the Musée Napoléon and granted France a constitution; he was not an entire failure. HB's preface was signed not by any name but by 'THE SOLDIER WHOM YOU [Napoleon] BUTTONHOLED AT GÖRLITZ'. This historic meeting in Silesia is relatively undocumented: but history is ignorant of many things.[65]

Instead of dedicating the *History* to Napoleon, he later wondered whether it would not be better to dedicate it 'to sensitive souls', those lucky people who always seem to be in a minority. But, even fallen, the Emperor remains the magnetic north of the work. It was he who had respected Leonardo's almost ruined *Last Supper* enough to forbid his soldiers from stabling their horses in the refectory of Santa Maria delle Grazie: for that alone, HB promoted Napoleon to the rank of Renaissance Man. His 'despotic government' had made great art possible again. But, even more than an enlightened despot, what the world needed now was writers. 'What is in itself more paltry than the little bit of metal called a printer's character? It topples tyrants from their thrones.' HB's friend Louis Crozet was horrified at his friend's *audace*, and told him not to run too many risks with the censorship. One of the things that most enraged HB was the need for *The History of Painting* to be published in *ancien régime* spelling, with imperfect endings in '-oit' instead of the more modern '-ait'. It remains a quirky, pioneering work, filled with information that seems irrelevant to painting (but is not). If Vasari had been loosely translated by Voltaire, then expanded and footnoted by Burckhardt and Baedeker, the result would still have had absolutely nothing in common with HB's *History of Painting in Italy*.

Angels, haloes, and blood

There is something Pagan in me that I cannot shake off.
In short, I deny nothing, but doubt everything.
Lord Byron

On 16th October 1815 HB fought '**a great battle**', presumably
with Angela. A little later that month he noted, 'One must adore
the ECHO,' a Pythagorean maxim counselling withdrawal from
public life in times of political unrest. The rest of his diary for the
memorable year 1815 is a series of observations unusually disjointed, even by HB's standards. On 1st December, Angela wrote
him a fierce letter in Italian, telling him she would no longer see
him: 'Your behaviour towards me is such that I can no longer feel
for you either love or friendship [...] From this time on we are
dead to each other!' She signed it 'Luigia Cerami', a fictitious
first name and a surname plausibly interpreted by Stendhal
scholar Victor Del Litto as an Italian transcription of 'cher ami'
– HB's pseudonymity was obviously contagious. HB scribbled
a note on the letter: 'Dismissed 1st December 1815. Cost 4,000
francs. Costs 4,000 francs more than an ordinary dancer at 200 fr.
per month.' His scribble may or may not have referred to
Angela.

In Milan HB had again started to frequent the Scala, and was
admitted to the *loge* of Lodovico di Breme, a leading liberal,
who introduced him to the patriots and romantics of Lombardy.

When Byron arrived in Milan, HB was duly presented to him in this very same *loge*: he was charmed by the young Lord's beautiful, expressive, noble eyes, his '**charming angel's** profile'. HB placed Lord Byron, together with Napoleon and Canova, in the first rank of men he had known; Byron was 'the greatest living poet'. (Colomb wrote: 'Beyle shared something of [Byron's] rebellion against modern civilisation; that was probably the secret of his bond with Byron.') HB later became disenchanted with His Lordship's demeanour, his *hauteur* and his pose as an aristocratic dandy. *Don Juan* interested HB, more for its attack on cant than for its eponymous hero, and he borrowed many of his epigraphs from Byron's work. But the two writers later had an epistolary quarrel about Walter Scott. Byron wrote to HB in May 1823; he mentioned the fate of Silvio Pellico, a friend of HB's since 1816 who had been arrested in the wave of repression that overwhelmed Milan in 1820. Pellico had been sentenced to death and then sent, instead, to the Spielberg prison in Moravia where he was now languishing. 'Poor Pellico! I trust that, in his iron solitude, his Muse is consoling him in part,' Byron wrote. But the main burden of his letter was his demurral at HB's dismissal of Scott. 'With his politics I have nothing to do,' said Byron; but, 'I say that Walter Scott is as nearly a thorough good man as man can be.' HB's reply was fierce. Who cared whether Scott was 'a good man' or not? And was he all that good? He highlighted the political issue that Byron had marginalised. 'You are thereby refusing to take into consideration precisely the thing that makes me regard the character of the illustrious Scot [i.e., Scott], as *hardly worthy of enthusiasm. Private virtues are not very difficult in a man who has the pleasure of making himself rich, nor are they rare, nor worthy of any great esteem.'* Scott was the opposite of Pellico, who was suffering for his convictions (and unlikely to be much visited by his Muse in the grim conditions of the Spielberg); Scott was a shrewd politician who had feathered his own nest; he was hoping for a baronetcy or a peerage in

Scotland; he was not 'crazy' enough to be a real writer – so HB informed Byron.[66] HB had initially acclaimed Scott's work: it had helped to promote Romanticism, it had overcome the artificiality of eighteenth-century writing by restoring 'the rights of nature', and Scott was (as HB did not aspire to be) a master of vivid description. But HB was alienated by what he saw as Scott's political conservatism. When Scott wrote a biography of Napoleon, HB was stung (a *Tory*... writing about Napoleon!) and denounced the work for its countless mistakes. He then, of course, drew on it extensively for his own *Memoirs of Napoleon*.

As well as angels such as the youngish Byron, HB was at this time taking an interest in saints: he speculated that the halo with which they were depicted in art was perhaps the effect of friction, as in the case of Spanish monks who wear flannel next to their skin and are insulated from their surroundings: the continual friction of their robes sends the 'electrical fluid' up to their heads, and on cold, dry days they will naturally appear encircled by a halo.

In 1816 HB was being bled frequently for his 'plethora' of blood. He suffered from palpitations or 'nervous beatings of the artery'. On 9th March 1816, '**I thought of death this morning.**' A medical consultation in July of this year reveals that HB had suffered from his first attack of VD in 1800 and then two severe attacks in 1809 and 1810; that in December 1814 he had self-medicated for an episode of depression by consuming great quantities of zabaglione and coffee; and that he was prone to palpitations, numbness and fits of weakness which made him anxious that he might collapse in the street. He came from a family that suffered from nerves; HB's own 'nervous sensibility' was 'aroused to a morbid degree'. The patient – we learn – had withdrawn to Italy after the fall of Napoleon so as not to succumb to gloom; here he read and studied to excess. His symptoms were alleviated by a pleasant visitor, and aggravated by bores.

Some time in 1816, his German love, Mina von Griesheim, whose husband had died in the war, withdrew as a canoness to the Convent of the Holy Virgin in Minden.

In 1817 HB was in Rome, Naples, Milan, Grenoble, Paris, England, Paris, Grenoble, Milan… In Rome, on his thirty-fourth birthday (23rd January), he visited the Sistine Chapel, a place that constantly drew him back.

London

It was a Sunday afternoon, wet and cheerless; and a duller
spectacle this earth of ours has not to show than a rainy
Sunday in London.

Thomas de Quincey

HB arrived in London on 3rd August 1817. John Rennie's toll
bridge had recently opened and was already officially known as
'Waterloo Bridge', though the public preferred the old name,
since here (wrote HB), 'The military spirit is not regarded as the
sole depositary of national glory.' (The bridge was painted that
year from Whitehall stairs, under a louring grey sky, by John
Constable.) 'Milan everywhere', noted HB: this was a code name
designed either by himself or by one of his travelling companions
to refer to Napoleon, still casting a shadow on victorious Albion
(and in fact, now that he was safely out of the way, admired by
many of the English). Just before dinner in Leicester Square, one
evening, HB saw the great panorama of the Battle of Waterloo:
although disinclined (he thought) to patriotism, he was a little
saddened by the sight of this great defeat (though he agreed that
it *did* give a good impression of what a battle was like). In St
Paul's he found most of the statues (admirals, generals) heavy
and sometimes ridiculous, but that of Samuel Johnson, 'attractive
and philosophical', was rather good. He saw children being
carried home by their parents, a 'remarkable phenomenon' that

tended to prove the happiness of English domestic life. The English were, however, quite rough and ready in their manners. The men would not hesitate to grab a map out of your hands. The women brushed their 'most secret charms' against you in the theatre, and the breasts of even decent ladies in the street were on show, 'wobbling like jellies'. (Less decent ladies asked him *'Voulez-vous foutre moi?'*) But they were much taller than most French women, and had attractively long necks.

Oxford Street at nine in the evening was admirable, with well-lit streets leading off it: better than Paris! Conversely, over twenty works of theology per week were published in London: more than in Italy! 'Apparently, theologians sweat blood and water to reconcile the reason of the modern world [*la raison du siècle*] with the old fictions in the Hebrew poems.' Sundays were stiflingly boring – but this gave HB time to write his newspaper articles (reviews for the English press) in Green Park, where children sailed their little yachts across the pond.[67] He went to an excellent parody of the Don Juan story at the Surrey Theatre: the *Commendatore* interrupted his duel to put on a pair of glasses; and, when he died, he carefully blew out his candle. London's soldiers were not much in evidence, its watchmen (the only real police) were peaceable types who let people do what they wanted (which caused huge traffic jams when audiences poured out of the theatres). HB noted that 'no armed force is allowed to pass Temple Bar without written permission from the Lord Mayor'. After a visit to the Opera, where one of his companions, Gustave, picked up a prostitute in the gloomy foyer, the party took a fiacre to Soho Square and went upstairs into a very clean room, where the girl was told to strip. She said, '**I can not go to bed before you pay me my compliment.**' This consisted in a one-pound banknote. During the ensuing activity, she told her paramour, '**You make me so hot.**' The men then returned to the foyer, where they refreshed themselves with a cup of tea. It was indeed stiflingly hot and Gustave was starting to lose his temper; all of a sudden, his eyes fell on the 'nymph' who had just entertained him: she had come back to the theatre, 'fresher than ever'.

They found it difficult to gain admission to museums. In France, a mere passport sufficed. Édouard implored the Cerberus stationed at the door of knowledge, 'What do you think *these two extremely distinguished men of letters will say about the English nation?*' The Cerberus replied, 'Rules is rules, and they is *happarently* meant to be followed.' England was (of course) a paradox: the land of freedom and of cant, of brazen prostitution and of stifling Puritanism. HB started to suspect that these contradictions provided the English with a coiled energy that would propel these vanquishers of Napoleon to world domination, but at what a cost! Even without the savage trauma of empire, there was already the abominable work ethic, the joyless accumulation of capital, the spleen of the gloomy *milords*, the increasing suffering of the industrial working classes... Even HB's most off-the-cuff remarks about an England basking in its victory over Boney were acutely prophetic: this dumpy French tourist, with his paunch and his carefully dyed toupee and sideburns, eyeing up the ladies of Soho and fascinated by every inflection of voice, every actorly gesture, in a performance of *Othello*, also had the X-ray eyes of a Karl Marx (or a William Blake) seeing through the domination and exploitation inherent in post-war British society.

Metilde

The habitual state of my life: being unhappily in love,
loving music and painting, i.e. enjoying the products of
these arts and not clumsily indulging in them myself.
HB

In 1817, HB fell out with his sister Pauline. She had come to stay
with him in Italy; her presence made his heart grow less fond of
his *'cara sorella'*. He advised her to settle down as a schoolmarm.
She eventually found a job in the thermal baths of Enghien-les-
Bains, north of Paris, before dying in poverty back in Grenoble.
Il mondo è una bestia.

In 1818, in Milan, HB was working on a *Life of Napoleon*,
cribbing much of the material from *The Edinburgh Review*, and
becoming increasingly active in Milanese intellectual circles,
especially those in which opposition to Restoration Europe was
being discreetly but insistently voiced. One of the doctors who
treated him for his various ailments was the celebrated *philosophe*
and comrade-in-arms of the poet Ugo Foscolo, Giovanni Rasori,
who had just been released from prison, where he had spent
time for attending an anti-Austrian meeting. HB described him
as being 'as poor as Job, as gay as a lark [or as merry as a chaf-
finch, as they say in French], as great as Voltaire'.

And in March of that year, momentously, he was introduced to
Metilde Dembowski (née Viscontini). '4 March [1818]. Beginning

of a great musical phrase' – so we read in *Henry Brulard*.[68] He wrote in his diary, '**The 29th March he has had** a powerful thrust to the depths of his heart, one which confirms the things **in which** he is timid.' Metilde had slender lips, 'big eyes, melancholy and shy', and 'the loveliest forehead' with dark brown hair parted in the middle. Aged twenty-eight, she was the mother of two sons, Carlo and Ercole. Ten years before HB met her, she had married Jan Dembowski, a member of the Polish Legion incorporated into the army of Napoleon; the Emperor made him a baron. In spite of this, when Napoleon fell, Dembowski made overtures to the Austrians. Although Metilde had apparently married him against the wishes of her family, the romance – though it produced a child within nine months of their wedding – was soon loveless, and Metilde accused her husband openly of mistreatment. She was distressed when, during a period of separation, Dembowski briefly attempted to kidnap Ercole from the house of his in-laws, where the boy was staying. She settled in Milan, resenting (and yet dependent on) the protection of the Austrian military governor of Milan, Count Bubna von Littitz (who treated her well, thereby earning HB's profound gratitude) while maintaining relationships with Italian patriots plotting an end to the Austrian domination of Lombardy.

We know relatively little about HB's relationship with her, since he alludes to it in some of his most cryptic notes, sometimes in marginalia, often in his usual coded abbreviations. '**Battle and defeat of 29th March on Me's bancks**' – 'My' banks? Metilde's benches? Did a fumbling attempt at seduction go wrong? (This note he made in his copy of *The History of Painting*.) Or '*Affaire de San Francisco* against **bash**' – probably bashfulness: but if so, what does San Francisco, or St Francis, have to do with it? Sometimes biographers are reduced to scratching their heads over such minimal annotations as '***The My***' in the margin of a copy of Montesquieu. Why '***The My***'? How do we even know (if we do) that this has anything to do with Metilde?

The different stages of the traditional love affair as analysed by HB in *On Love* were zipped through in record time: everything crystallised with remarkable speed, at least on his side. By Christmastime 1818 he was so much in love he could no longer work, no longer read. 6th January 1819, diary, '**I am without witt and very** tender.' She was as beautiful as a *Herodias* by Leonardo.[69] She was endowed with Spanish nobility of soul. She was '**the greatest event of his life**' – at least, these were the words he wrote on the cover of a copy of *Macbeth*.

But there was no crystallisation on her side. Her initial friendliness was replaced by growing distance. HB's despair grew. Some of his diary entries are addressed to her ('I was punished, as I left, for having paid attention to something other than you'), or contain drafts of phrases to use in letters to her. By October 1818 he was writing to her, 'I am really unhappy, it seems to me that each day I love you more and that you no longer have for me the simple friendship that you used to show.' Proof of his love, he said, lay in the '*gaucherie*' with which he was overcome every time they were together: 'As soon as I set eyes on you, I tremble.' He even translated the beginning of this letter into Italian for her – paradoxically enough, since she understood French perfectly well. Perhaps he needed another language in which to express the self-dispossession of love? But his feelings were probably impossible to express in either French or Italian. From Varese he wrote (but did he send the letter? – we have only his rough drafts) that he was surrounded by bourgeois folk, noisy and practical, unaffected by his amorous melancholy (and yet, he surmised, just as unhappy as he was). The greatest pleasure he can enjoy, he says, is counting the days until he sees her again – a month – thirty whole days! He has found a little consolation in Varese's hilltop church of Santa Maria del Monte, a place of pilgrimage since the fifteenth century, with its five Chapels of the Majestic Mysteries and its view over the lake to the distant Alps. He remembers the music he heard here once. In his own notebooks he wrote despondently, and repeatedly, 'I love her too much to work,' even though he needed to, being (as ever) short of cash. Even Rossini's music gave him only ambiguous pleasure. *Armida*, which he heard in La Scala, was hot stuff – 'it will give you a ten-day erection': but this was not necessarily a recommendation, especially if there was nowhere to put the said erection.[70] On 12th May 1819, only five and a half hours after Metilde had left Milan, he sat down and wrote, asking what on earth he was going to do for the next forty days. He was still struck incoherent with passion and timidity in her presence, he acknowledged. 'Do I have to find myself so inferior to myself and so *dumb*?' he lamented.

She had taken herself off to visit her sons, who were at boarding school in Volterra. This attractive small town[71] had been conquered by Florence in the Renaissance; it had been under the control of the Medici (who built a prison) and then of the Grand Dukes of Florence. It is celebrated for the beautiful plaques bearing the devices of various noble families, displayed on the walls of the Palazzo dei Priori in the splendid town square. Here HB arrived, three weeks later, having taken the precaution of disguising himself with a pair of green spectacles (they would also shield his eyes from the radiant beauty of the stern Madonna, the Volteranno Sibyl, whom he was now planning to stalk). There she was, on her way home from visiting her sons, practically the first person he saw on arrival: she didn't recognise him, but later that evening she spotted him just as he was taking his glasses off, and the following day, while she was out walking *extra muros*, there he was again, quite by chance – or so he claimed in his letter of 7th June. On the draft of this letter, too, with its excuses and its pleas ('Love me, if you will, divine Metilde, but, in God's name, do not despise me'), he jotted down some bitter reflections: 'The idea of dropping it all' and 'Jealousy for signor Giorgi' (a potential rival), and his own version of *così fan tutte*: 'Honest women, just as dishonest [*coquines*] as the dishonest ones.' But he left Volterra 'drunk with joy' since she had not actually rejected him for good.

Back in Milan, however, his assiduity made her feel he was compromising her: she restricted his visits to once a fortnight (in his diary, '**I wrote Love, and see her only every fornight**' [sic]; he had asked to see her four times a month). She even asked him to cut down the number of letters he wrote to her. HB suffered horribly from jealousy. His diary for 1819 ends with a list of dates detailing in particular the occasions when he had seen Metilde.[72]

Perhaps the saddest love letter that has been preserved from this period (they addressed each other, in their letters, as 'Monsieur' and 'Madame') is also one of the briefest, dated 8th July 1820. He thanks Metilde for some pretty views of Switzerland that she had sent him from a stay in Berne. He writes, 'I had despised that country ever since 1815, because of the barbarous way our poor exiled liberals had been treated there. I was altogether disenchanted. The sight of those beautiful mountains that you were able to see […] has reconciled me somewhat with it.' Even in the throes of love, he could not avoid allusions to politics.

Then the last letter, to be sent 3rd January 1821, asking to see her 'for a quarter of an hour, one of these evenings. I feel crushed by melancholy.' She need fear no indiscretion on his part. 'I will not claim any right to speak to you; I will be *aimable*.' He signed it 'D.', perhaps for 'Dominique'.

While Dembowski was away at the wars, Metilde may already have had an affair with Ugo Foscolo, the Italian poet who had been taught by Cesarotti, translator of 'Ossian', that band of Scotch mist that settled over literary Europe at the end of the eighteenth century. Foscolo at first hailed Napoleon as a liberator; but instead of bringing liberty to Venice, the Emperor signed the Treaty of Campo Formio, which delivered it into the hands of the Austrians. Foscolo continued to put his hopes in Napoleon, but the traumatic effect that political upheavals could have on a sensitive mind is portrayed in his novel *Last Letters of Jacopo Ortis*, which HB praised in his *Italy in 1818*. Foscolo was a liberal, an Italian patriot, and an inspiration to the *carbonari*. These were patriots who longed for Italian unification; they were hostile to

Murat under Napoleon and to the Austrians after Napoleon's fall, and were now becoming increasingly active. It is unclear how much HB's passion for Metilde was inspired by her increasingly ardent nationalism. The political atmosphere in Italy was by now very tense. Southern Europe was increasingly rebellious; there were uprisings in Spain in 1820, Naples in July of that year, and Piedmont in the following spring. HB was an object of suspicion – to the liberals (usually Italian patriots) because he was a Frenchman, to the Austrians because he was a liberal. Friends had been avoiding him, salon doors had not opened with their usual alacrity to receive him: this man of many names who seemed unable to speak without irony or *persiflage* was suspected of being a spy. Who was he working for? When HB was informed by his old friend Plana, now an astronomer in Turin, that many of his former friends thought he was working for the French government, he was more shocked and wounded than at any other time in his life. Many of his friends from Milan's liberal salons were arrested; some were condemned to death, though the sentence was usually commuted to imprisonment, exile, or permanent police surveillance. He admired their idealism; he hesitated to endorse some of their less realistic plans. Either way, he described the Austrian repression that ensued as a 'terror'.

On 15th May 1821, Napoleon died in St Helena. Reading the news, HB felt 'a profound sorrow, mingled with admiration'.

On 7th June 1821, he left Metilde for the last time. He was convinced that she secretly shared his feelings and had merely been dissuaded from yielding to him by the malicious gossip of the aptly named Madame Traversi, her cousin. And he had decided that life amid the political agitations of Milan was too stressful. One of the arrested conspirators, perhaps thinking that by naming HB he would draw the police off the scent of more authentic and more vulnerable plotters, called HB 'extremely dangerous', and a police report of the time calls him 'irreligious, revolutionary, an enemy of the legitimate authority'. On 13th June 1821, 'I leave Milan **with** despair for Basle and Paris.'

He passed through Airolo, Bellinzona, Lugano: ten years later, the mere mention of these place-names filled him with a shudder. He could not walk because of his venereal disease: and, even though he had been a sub-lieutenant of cavalry in the 6th dragoons for nearly a year (1800–1), he claimed that he was always falling off horses.[73] But he insisted on riding over the Alps: 'I descend the Saint-Gothard Pass without putting a foot to the ground, in the hope of tumbling down into some gorge.' Only in Altdorf did a kitschy statue of William Tell calm him down a little. After all, if Metilde loved political freedom more than she loved HB, he was sharing in that love by loving political freedom too.[74] Either way, Tell, that hero of liberty, was one of his heroes, especially since the 'ministerial hacks' of every country continued to claim that no such man had ever existed.

On Christmas Eve, 1822, Metilde was taken in for questioning by the Austrian police, apparently because of her suspected links with the *carbonari*, many of whom were again being sent to the Spielberg. She treated her interrogators with dignified disdain. She gave away nothing.

HB had 3,500 francs left: maybe, once he'd run through it, he would blow his brains out. But 'political curiosity' kept him alive. In Paris he tried to conceal the feelings that had ravaged his heart, but he doodled little pictures of pistols into the margin of his works. He continued to see Metilde everywhere: a line of rocks he had seen on the road from Dole to Arbois had mimicked her shape. He even saw her once in a brothel in Paris – at least in his mind's eye. He and his friends went there one August day: Mareste was the first to enjoy the dark-eyed, Titianesque Alexandrine, a girl of seventeen or eighteen. Then it was HB's turn: but he found that, even after ten minutes contemplating her as she lay stretched on the bed, he was impotent. He had suddenly thought of Metilde. His friends roared with laughter; he, as usual, was too interested in his own reactions to be unduly bothered. He freely discussed these occasional crises of masculinity with Mérimée, pointing out that 'an adroit hand, an officious tongue', not to mention 'a fine Portuguese dildo in rubber, properly attached to your belt', were perfectly adequate substitutes. But the word 'fiasco' became part of his vocabulary, referring to a failure in performance consequent upon an excess of desire. When at long last he was able to visit the philosopher he so much admired, Destutt de Tracy, he found himself tongue-tied: 'complete fiasco', he noted. The fiasco is a sign of vulnerability, a token of the failure of human calculation, and a presentiment of something deeper (love, for instance). His friends made him a '*babilan*' (his own name for an impotent man) and swapped letters in which the attempts of this *sodomist* to marry were mocked. At this point heterosexual male critics usually point out, with relief, that HB had already proved his abilities in bed and, after his flop with Alexandrine, later restored the honour of his sex with Alberthe de Rubempré. Such distasteful gossip need not detain us here: every man has a right to his private life.[75]

A certain M. Rapture *always* suffered from 'fiascos', and told HB so in Messina: but HB wisely remarked, in *On Love*, that Rapture was as much of a man as any other, and had had two charming mistresses.

In autumn 1823, HB was again in London, led there by his 'love of Shakespeare' and 'his liking for great trees': he particularly admired those in Richmond Park, where he sat reading Lucy Hutchinson's memoirs of her Parliamentarian husband. He saw Kean playing Richard II and Othello, and with his friends went to another brothel, this time in Lambeth; the English ladies (doll-like, pale, oddly dainty in their tiny house with its tiny garden) and their French customers celebrated what was later to be known as the *Entente cordiale* by drinking both tea and champagne. Soon HB, relieved that he had not been robbed or murdered overnight (London south of the river was already a dodgy place, especially the Lambeth area), was contributing to the *English Magazine*, in which he kept his readers informed of the latest developments in Continental literature.

The thieving magpie

A few shrewd kicks *a posteriori* might have made Rossini
a better composer.
Beethoven

In 1823 HB turned forty. In a later diary entry signed
'Dominique', he wrote, 'Events don't affect you any more after
forty.' Indeed, from about this time his diary entries become
much more cursory (not only because he was in his forties,
but because his writing energies were finding other outlets). He
wrote *Racine and Shakespeare*, a manifesto in favour of the latter against the former (a taste for Shakespeare was an essential
ingredient in the burgeoning Romantic school in France); a first
version was published in 1823, and it was revised and issued as
a pamphlet (a more deliberately polemical form) in 1825.[76] The
efficient cause of the work had been the way a Paris audience
had rowdily mocked an English company of actors performing Shakespeare. HB was defending, as so often, the foreign
against the French, and the new against the old. He decreed
simply that Romanticism was what gave the 'greatest possible
pleasure' to a contemporary audience, here and now; classicism
was for granddads. And by 'new' he meant 'really new', not the
retro-chic designer-Catholicism of Chateaubriand with its nostalgia for the feudal Middle Ages, all ruins, gloom, transience
and renunciation. He also wrote a *Life of Rossini*, a beautifully

composed set of variations on the usual *Beylist* themes, with some splendid *fioriture*. It details how HB once met a thirty-year-old man in an inn at Terracina, south of Rome. Here HB started to sing the praises of Rossini. His interlocutor suddenly blushed and seemed embarrassed – and HB realised that, yes, it was the great Rossini himself. Years later, in London, the two men happened to be in the same room. Someone pointed out HB to Rossini, whose face went blank. Surely the musician had met his biographer before? 'This is the first time I've ever set eyes on him,' said the great composer, no doubt afflicted by the amnesia that overcame so many of HB's acquaintances. (Rossini even later forgot this very same London meeting – and was 'furious' at HB's biography of him, as its author had known he would be.[77]) HB's comments on music continued to distress its professional practitioners: Berlioz thought they were just 'stupid'.

In his forties, HB became an habitué of some of the liveliest salons in Paris. Not, however, those of writers such as Victor Hugo: the two met, unsheathed their claws at each other, hissed, spat, and parted; Hugo later said that HB was witty but idiotic; HB had written that Hugo's verse was 'soporific'. Nor those of aristocrats (he would never have gained access to the Faubourg Saint-Germain). Rather, the salons he attended were mainly those of artists, scholars, and scientists. Thus it is in a letter from the botanist Adrien de Jussieu to the historian and travel writer Jean-Jacques Ampère (son of the father of the amp), describing the salon of the great biologist Cuvier, that we learn of an HB who is always amusing, never admiring, sometimes devious ('candour is not really in his character') – a 'plump Mephistopheles'. HB also adopted another current description of himself as a 'fat butcher': it was his enormous sideburns that had earned him this sobriquet (though the way he could stick the knife into pomposity and pretentiousness may also have contributed to the image). An unflattering portrait of him, labelled 'La Belle Stendhal en 1827', appeared on Nevers plate and showed him as a dandified, balding, simian figure with a top hat and a furled umbrella. His ambitions to become a second Molière now assumed a new form; he decided that 'the pamphlet is the comedy of the present age', and poured his gifts for satire into *Racine and Shakespeare* or his polemics against the industrious Saint-Simonians.[78]

On 22nd May 1824, Clémentine Curial ('Menti') became his mistress. In his diary he wrote the word 'Gúerison', for 'cure': at last he was cured of his love for Metilde. But he continued to think of her 'ten times a week, and often for two hours at a time'. He broke with Clémentine at the end of May 1826, after some falling out between them – 'the deepest misfortune **of his life**' – just as he was about to embark for England. She had been one of the few women to reciprocate his affections, at times too insistently – though she also thought he was a bad boy, who only wanted her for her body. He rewrote *Rome, Naples and Florence in 1817*. He was always critical of his more 'factual' works. 26th December: 'Reading my works makes me sad. It seems to remind one of a long-dead passion.' 28th December: '*The History of Painting* is unintelligible, too short, too concise, too dense.' Maybe: but its more enthusiastic readers included Delacroix, Baudelaire – and Cézanne, who claimed to have read it three times. And he was not so diffident about it as he claimed; he had long since arranged for copies of this *History of Painting* to be sent to Mme de Staël, Benjamin Constant, a considerable number of Counts, various contributors to *The Edinburgh Review*,[79] and 'milord Byron', c/o Murray, Publishers, London. Just to be on the safe side (Mme de Staël's work had been pulped on Napoleon's orders: he did not wish a French regime to sin against literature a second time), he asked for six hundred copies to be sent to places outside France, even though his book was essentially 'a work of mathematics' unlikely to attract attention except from a limited circle of cheerful souls.

In March 1825, a new and enlarged edition of *Racine and Shakespeare* went on sale in March. HB learned of Metilde's death (she died on 1st May, aged thirty-five, of consumption), and wrote in his copy of *On Love*, which had largely been inspired by his feelings for her, the words '1st May 1825. **Death of the auth.**' And yet HB's diary for mid-1825 is mute on the subject of Metilde's death. In the period 7th–11th May 1825, he wrote simply '7th–11th May 1825'. In July he mentioned that he was not very well and not very merry, but had seen a 'beauty' walking down the boulevard with a basket on her arm. He seems to have talked little about Metilde; indeed, Mérimée thought that HB had had only two '*amours-passions*' (HB's own term): Angela Pietragrua and Clémentine Curial. One evening in 1836, as HB and Mérimée walked under the great trees of Laon, with its fine cathedral, HB said that he had just met Clémentine again. She was forty-seven, and he was as much in love with her as ever. 'How can you love me at my age?' she asked. He proved that he did so; and his eyes were full of tears as he recounted this story to Mérimée. But Metilde? And yet, in his *Life of Henry Brulard*, he imagined her seeing his book from her present place, and feeling pleased that she was still remembered.

On a new plot against the industrialists is a pamphlet that HB wrote at the end of 1825. The 'plot' is his own; he denounces the new cult of 'productivity' so beloved of the Saint-Simonians; instead of praising hardworking people who make money, largely by making other people work even harder for much less money, he exalts both the life of leisure (essentially the apanage of the 'thinking class') and the spirit of self-sacrifice. His models are not rich bankers or factory owners (nor does he particularly dwell on the virtues of the proletariat), but rather the Italian revolutionary Santa-Rosa and Lord Byron, both of whom gave their lives for the liberty of Greece. This pamphlet shocked some on the left who were already placing their faith in the white heat of technology.

In 1826, HB – still suffering from his break-up with Clémentine – toured England, travelling as far north as Newcastle, the Lake District, Manchester, and Durham. His close friend Sutton

Sharpe, an enlightened lawyer who had known HB in the latter's circles in Paris, acted as his guide and introduced him to his own uncles, the Rogers, near Birmingham: on the whole, the acquaintances HB made in Britain were liberals or, as they were called on this side of the Channel, 'radicals'. He was increasingly convinced that the Industrial Revolution was turning Britain into a slave society, and ruining its countryside. He feared that the same would happen in France: 'Canals are finding their way across our fields, and melancholy into our salons.' He now finished *Armance*, about a young man, Octave, who refuses production (and reproduction); he is given every opportunity to marry his beloved Armance and yet shies away from it; when he does eventually marry, he tries to escape to Greece to fight the Turks, but this is only a pretext for a more self-destructive act. Why? HB told Mérimée that Octave suffered from impotence: however, by refusing to name Octave's condition, the novel enriches its potential readings – Octave's malady may be a signifier of something deeper, or not even a malady at all. The shadow of something beyond articulation falls on this text: Octave overcomes the obstacles to his love, but does he really want the prize he is granted?

Its first readers were generally flummoxed; *Le Figaro* thought that HB made salon life look like a madhouse full of raving lunatics.

On the last day of 1827, HB arrived in Milan. On the first day of 1828, he was ordered by the Austrian police to leave Austrian territory immediately. They told him that – in his words – 'all the learned' knew perfectly well that 'Stendhal' and 'Beyle' were synonyms. (He stayed on, rebelliously, for a good twelve hours. [80]) For the rest of the year, almost penniless, he tried to find a job and worked on a play called *Henri III*. (Dumas's play *Henri III and His Court* was first performed in February 1829: this was the great age of the historical drama, that unwieldy product of French Romanticism, full of local colour and emphatic movement, with its exploded dramatic unities, alexandrines bursting at the seams, and a large dose of hokum; the main merit of most of these plays was to have provided Verdi with several of his plots.)

The last diary entry of the year looks back to an earlier trauma: 'Mét[ilde] **in** Milan 1819: the greatest sorrow.' And then, immediately underneath, he repeats, 'Metilde in Milan in 1819.'

The Red and the Black

Art was always free of life, and its colour never reflected
the colour of the flag flying over the city's fortress.

Viktor Shklovsky

HB continued to view Restoration France with disdain, and
to brood on politics. In 1829, a diary note set out a minimalist
political programme: 'A government should provide, as cheaply
as possible: 1) *justice* between individuals, 2) *safety* in the streets
and on the roads, 3) coinage properly marked with its correct
value; 4) it must prosecute wars well. And that is all.' (Except
that, 'Everyone in France should pay for their priest the same
way as they pay for their doctor.')

In July of the revolutionary year 1830, Charles X fell and
went into exile; Louis-Philippe assumed the throne as a 'citizen
king'.[81] HB subtitled his novel *The Red and the Black* a 'Chronicle
of 1830', though in fact it alludes to the events of that year only
indirectly, and he had written a good half of it before the July
Days. HB was glad to see Charles X go (after all, as the Count
d'Artois, the future Charles X had been the man who bestowed
the Cross of the Legion of Honour on Chérubin Beyle), but
thought that Charles had been allowed to escape too lightly;
the French had missed the opportunity for another fine royal
guillotining, or at least the removal of the heads of His Majesty's
chief ministers. This would only have been fair. After all, it had

been under the rule of Charles X that, in April 1825, the law on sacrilege had been introduced. Anyone who profaned a consecrated host in public was to be sentenced to death; his right hand was to be severed before he was executed.[82] Even the religious establishment found this measure a little excessive. Eventually, amputation was replaced by a simple *amende honorable* in front of the church, and the culprit was allowed to be executed with his hands intact.

While correcting the proofs of the first part of *The Red and the Black*, HB followed the revolution of 28th–30th July 1830 (days of hot sunshine and smoke-filled skies), but did not participate in them. The printers were on strike anyway, so his book could not be published just yet. On 28th July he sat at home while the 'battle of Paris' raged between one and two o'clock. The *peuple* in the rue Rameau, beneath his window, showed considerable bravery as they were fired at by the 'Jesuits'.[83] He ventured down to the Palais-Royal: 'I saw the bullets under the pillars of the Théâtre-Français, with very little danger on my part' – though an insurgent next to him was shot dead. But he felt no urge to join the uprising: he just went home and carried on reading the *Memorial of Saint-Helena*, perched in his apartment like Julien Sorel on a beam up in the sawmill, in a *tête-à-tête* with his hero.[84]

The Red and the Black details the rise and fall of Julien Sorel, a rebellious plebeian who cannot mimic his hero Napoleon by rising through the ranks of the army (though why this should be so difficult remains unclear; France still had an army in the 1820s, and in 1830 would embark on the colonisation of Algeria; a colonial career might well have brought Julien the glory he craved). Instead, he channels his revolt into subversive hyperconformity, training as a priest and rising to the point where he is on the verge of marrying into the aristocracy that he had earlier despised. But a pistol shot undoes him; his mistake was partly to think that his novel was finished once he had achieved his ambition, and that all the credit belonged to him alone. He discovers that he is not the hero of his own narrative, but of somebody else's; his rise has been helped by many *adjuvants*, mainly women, but also by Fortune, a much-maligned lady. He is allowed, at the end, to realise that what had been valuable in his life had little to do with power or control; it was more a matter of playing with the woman he loves and her children in the garden. However, it is impossible to draw a lesson of political quietism from the novel. Only because he had wanted to be a Napoleon does Julien now see that chasing butterflies was actually much more fun. If he had done nothing but chase butterflies, he would probably still be thoroughly frustrated. He has had to learn his lesson only when it is too late to apply it; a common phenomenon. But the lesson, although impracticable, is still learned. The book ends with various deaths and a lavish, nocturnal, candle-lit mountain-side funeral attended by a score of priests, a *grande dame* scattering thousands of five-franc coins to the local peasants, and a burial in a cave where innumerable candles shed their gleam on expensive funerary marbles brought from Italy.

There have been several successful film versions of the novel, and a fine BBC adaptation (1993), starring Ewan MacGregor and the lovely Rachel Weisz – an effective rewrite of Woody Allen's *Play it Again, Sam*, with Napoleon playing Humphrey Bogart.

On 6th August 1830 HB imagined a dialogue between himself and Guizot (soon to be appointed Minister of the Interior) in which he discussed the possibility of obtaining a Prefecture under the new regime – maybe in Quimper. He issued, albeit in the privacy of his diary, a 'proclamation' to his fellow citizens ('The illustrious prince who is at the head of our new and youthful liberty...[85] I come among you to hasten the flourishing of your institutions and to guide your efforts... Devoted to the fundamental law, the Prince, and the National Guard, I will support, with all the strength at my disposal, the great movement that is happening in France', etc.: he added a footnote reminding himself to 'tone down the republican slant'). It was signed as from

Quimper, 11th August 1830, by 'Prefect of Finistère Beyle'. He sketched out possible lines to take in an interview with Guizot, and pondered whether he ought to start going to mass, and whether he should consult the men of the extreme left or the centre left, or both. And he drew up a shopping list:

Toupee
False teeth
Umbrella
Black cravats
Three pairs of boots
The uniform of a National Guard (fifty-five francs)
Etc.

… as well as a list of people to see and questions to ask on arrival, such as: Who are the most reactionary men in town? The four most liberal? The four wealthiest? The four wittiest? The four prettiest women? And which are the wickedest priests?

A strange note at the end of Part II, ch. 13 of *The Red and the Black* reads as follows: 'Wit los. Pref. gui. 11 A. 30' which, being interpreted, means 'Being witty lost me a prefecture under Guizot on 11th August 1830.'[86] And so, on 25th September he was appointed, not to a Prefecture, but to a French consulate, not in Leghorn, as he had thought, but in Trieste. Before leaving Paris, he wrote a letter to the *Globe* (which he seems not to have sent[87]) suggesting what the new coat of arms of France might be. All heraldic beasts, he noted, were already taken: Spain had the lion, the eagle recalled 'dangerous thoughts' (of 'Milan', i.e. Napoleon), the farmyard cockerel was too humble. He suggested that the arms of France could now simply be the number '29', in honour of 29th July, a date which already had a patina of ancient heroism.

The journey from Udine to Trieste passed very quickly. 'Strange view of the sky in the sea, immensely deep, on the right; lights. It's Trieste.' On 6th November he proposed marriage to

Giulia Rinieri, who had been his mistress since 22nd March ('You're old and ugly,' she charmingly told him, before kissing him). The marriage did not take place. On 4th December he was told that the Austrian authorities were refusing to allow HB, aka 'M. de Standhol' [sic] to take up his post in Trieste. He was, and was not, Consul for about four months – an uneasy period in which he belonged nowhere, but just enough time to fall for the charms of 25-year-old Caroline Ungher, who had sung in the premiere of Beethoven's Ninth.

Cityold

Since the papal government requires from its subjects
little more than the payment of taxes and regular
attendance at mass, it presents fewer obstacles to the
luxuriant growth and energy of the passions than do
the better-regulated governments of France and England.
Stendhal, Life of Rossini

Finally, on 11th February 1831, Louis-Philippe ('the most rascally
of **Kings**') signed a paper saying that, having been informed
of the 'intelligence, probity, zeal and fidelity to our service of
M. Marie-Henri Beyle', he had chosen the said M. Beyle to be
French Consul at Civitavecchia. This is a seaside town in Latium,
lying between the rivers Mignone in the north and Marangone
in the south. It was an Etruscan settlement, and became a real
Roman town under Trajan, around 107 AD.

Its Latin name was Centumcellae ('a thousand cells').

Conquered by the Saracens in 828 (they held it for only a few
years), the town passed from Byzantine hands at the end of the
ninth century, becoming one of the Papal States. By the time
HB was sent there as Consul, it had long been Rome's principal
port. It had a huge fortress partly designed by Michelangelo, and
completed in the reign of Pope Paul III (Alessandro Farnese).
HB's nickname for Civitavecchia was 'Abeille' ('Bee'), because of
its Barberini tower – the coat of arms of the Barberini was a bee

– though he also translated its name into Beylish, as '**Cityold**'. None of these interesting details compensated for the fact that, having escaped the provincial hole of Grenoble and lived in some of the most exciting cities in Europe (Paris, Vienna, Berlin…), HB had ended up in yet another provincial hole. A French visitor, M. de Gasparin, a former Minister of the Interior, agreed with him that you needed to have murdered both father and mother to deserve being exiled to this dump of a place, with its 7,400 inhabitants. Its one redeeming feature was that it lay only fifty miles from Rome – an overnight journey (during the daytime the trip carried the traveller through a scrubby, unhealthy, monotonous landscape). HB hated the 'self-important air' he had to assume, the interest he had to feign in official letters. 'In my view, there is nothing in the world more stupid than gravity.' Financially, he was better off than before, but he would have preferred the *bohème* back in the rue Saint-Roch, Paris. 'The animal's true profession is writing a novel in an attic – I prefer the pleasure of writing crazy nonsense to that of wearing an embroidered [*brodé*] suit costing 800 francs.' He continued to dream of a consulate elsewhere: Valencia, for example. Or a nice little library job back in Paris, despite his earlier failure to secure such a sinecure (he had even written, in his job application, that 'time, *edax rerum*, has quite modified my political opinions'). 'My soul is a fire; it languishes if it isn't aflame. I need three or four cubic feet of new ideas per day, the same way a steamboat needs coal.' His window was sixty feet above the sea; after working, he would gather together the bits of waste paper on his desk, stick them in an envelope and chuck them into the waves.

On a visit to Rome that summer, he received a copy of *The Red and the Black* from the printer's. He sat and read it through, in St Peter's – and claimed, in a letter to Alberthe de Rubempré, that the death of Símon Bolívar, 'El Libertador', in 1830 was caused not by tuberculosis, as claimed, but by his intense jealousy at the success of HB's novel. (It actually met with somewhat mixed reviews.) Meanwhile, the revolutionary impulse in France had not been entirely extinguished under Louis-Philippe: in 1831, the silk workers of Lyon rose in rebellion. The main weavers among them were called '*canuts*'; theirs was one of the first great agitations of the Industrial Revolution. Faced with falling wages and the obstinacy of manufacturers who clung to the principles of free enterprise, the silk-workers had little option but to gather in the Croix-Rousse and march into town. They carried a black flag – one of the first times this colour was associated with revolution and anarchy (the red flag had already been hoisted by the Jacobins in 1791). More than a hundred and sixty died, and more than four hundred were injured in the ensuing bloodshed.

Following these events from the relative tranquillity of Civitavecchia, HB grew increasingly prone to dwell on the past. Leaving Paris had meant leaving his position as an admired, if perplexing, author. After *The Red and the Black* HB, who had always been publi-shy, committed nothing to the printing presses apart from the *Memoirs of a Tourist* of 1838. Everything else was left in manuscript form, almost all unfinished.

In October, he admired the view from the Janiculum, '*without comparison* the finest view in Rome', looking towards Mount Albano and the tomb of Cecilia Metella. He later pretended that his vision of Rome at the beginning of *The Life of Henry Brulard* dated from such an autumnal vision, on 16th October 1832. This beginning is one of the most staggeringly beautiful *incipits* in literature. It is also full of misinformation, initially claiming that HB had been present at the Battle of Wagram, conflating the *Judith* of the Cavalièr d'Arpino with that of Domenichino, etc. It has something of the grandeur of Gibbon's account of the moment at which the idea of writing of the decline and fall of the city first started to his mind – except that HB is going to describe the decline and fall, not of Rome, but of Mr Myself, a decline that had, of course, started very young, with the death of his mother. It is a dream vision[88] in which memories from Livy are as powerfully intense as the modern cityscape. After all, as HB points out, on the Janiculum from which he is enjoying the panorama of the *caput mundi* stands the church of San Pietro in Montorio, in which for so many years a particular painting by Raphael was displayed, depicting an epiphany on a mountain, and significantly known as the *Transfiguration*.[89]

Sitting on the steps of San Pietro, he lets his mind wander: he is soon going to hit fifty, that age when a man starts to reflect on *what he has been*, and *what he is*, only to realise that, 'I would find it really rather difficult to say.' The work (unfinished) ends with an increasingly incoherent discussion of *amour fou* and *bonheur fou*. It is characteristic that, for HB, real love and real happiness are 'mad'. He increasingly felt that middle age could be assuaged only in memory and fantasy; otherwise it was a slow decline into decrepitude, a horror. He started noting his age indirectly: one year he turned $26 \times 2 + \sqrt{9}$. His tastes were more or less fixed; he made few, if any, new discoveries. The latest writing from France aroused, at least in private (for in public he was more diplomatic), indifference, boredom, even anger: George Sand, Balzac, Hugo, Eugène Sue…

Etruscan places

The austere medal
Unearthed by a ploughman
Reveals an emperor.
Gautier

His diary for 1830 ended with a '**history of his life**' in which he referred to 'Mina v[on] Valtheim' (he even misremembered her name!), dismissed the turbulent year 1815 with the words 'blackened paper', and – as he increasingly did – muddled his dates. He studied the manners and customs of the Romans and read Livy ('stupid when he describes battles, always trots out the same score of phrases') and started to join in the amateur excavations of the many Etruscan remains in and around Civitavecchia. He clambered on all fours down into the '2,700-year-old tombs' in the necropolis near Corneto, only to find that many of the great vases had been broken by the 'antiquaries' of the age of Trajan or by the Saracens of the Middle Ages. He wrote to Marshal Soult to inform him of the statues – some colossal, many of them really beautiful – found at Cerveteri, an ancient Etruscan city between Civitavecchia and Rome, and in HB's day a gloomy little place prone to swamp fever. HB became an enthusiastic amateur archaeologist (at that time, there were few professionals): he loved bronze medals of the Roman emperors – Augustus, an astute rascal, Tiberius, half-crazed by depression but still a great prince, and Trajan, the only figure (apart from Julius Caesar) comparable with Napoleon. HB had already purchased a bust of Tiberius from a dig in Naples and gazed into the 'beautiful eyes' of the man who had ruled over one hundred and twenty million subjects.[90] And when he and his fellow enthusiasts found a tomb that was still intact, he found himself gazing at:

> … a great dead man, dressed in all his apparel, a crown of gold on his skull; laurel leaves in gold are much lighter than paper. Soon everything falls into a very damp dust, almost mud, and you are reduced to fishing out the laurel leaves from the mud, with a pin. It's at least three thousand years old, and sends your thoughts vividly back to the time when the poems of Homer were in the same state as our *Bible*.[91]

He travelled widely through Italy, with breaks in Paris. While returning from one of these latter, in December 1833, he was travelling by steamer down the Rhône when he met George Sand and Alfred de Musset. He made no reference to this encounter in his diary, but Sand did write an account: HB had drunk too much, she said, and was witty but a bit coarse. She and Musset watched, fascinated, as HB, in top hat, greatcoat and fur-lined boots, kicked up his heels and danced round the table (Musset included a lively sketch drawing).[92]

In 1834 he started writing *Lucien Leuwen*, and continued it for fifteen months. Its address to the reader ends with the words, 'Adieu, friendly reader; make sure you do not spend your life hating and being afraid.' His three prefaces to the novel play politics with a vengeance, noting that the police may well prevent its publication and casting himself both as a republican enthusiast for Robespierre and as a man who desires the return of the Bourbons under 'Louis XIX'. He also casts aspersions on democracy and says he would hate having to live in New York. 'He [the author] prefers having to court M. Guizot to having to court his bootmaker.' Having thus drawn down on himself the potential wrath of most of the political tendencies in the France of his day, HB proceeds to write his most overtly political novel: a depiction of the machinations of the various different social cliques and castes in the July Monarchy. Its hero, Lucien Leuwen (a lion among men – or a 'lion' in the nineteenth-century French sense of being a dandy) falls in love with the woman (the chaste-looking Mme de Chasteller) in front of whose house he falls off his horse, twice. The novel as we have it ends with Lucien rebelling against the 'dryness' of Paris life and revelling in the Rousseauesque melancholy of Lake Geneva; his soul is now open to the arts, and he thinks of the pleasures of Milan, the Charterhouse of Pavia, Bologna, Florence, etc.

Back in the real world of **Cityold**, HB's diary for November 1834 consisted largely of weather reports (the sirocco in Civitavecchia gave him a headache). He also gave details of how many pages he had written each day. He loved figures (his tourist guide, *Walks In Rome*, is full of facts and figures about the height, length and width of the churches he visits), and took an accountant's view of his own productivity, in spite of his hostility to the quantitative mentality of Saint-Simonian technocrats. He also continued to be fascinated by the thuggishness of life in Italy. In the margin of a copy of *Walks in Rome*, he noted, 'Sunday, 6th April 34. Young girl murdered next to me. I run across, she is in the middle of the street and near her head a little lake of blood, one foot in diameter. This is what M. V. Hugo calls swimming in your own blood.' Although an ex-soldier, HB was far from being a violent man; but he found murder oddly exciting. Young Italian women continued to expire in pools of blood at his feet (or at least on the pavement near his Roman residence), their throats slit. One had a shapely leg; he was struck by the blood that had spattered her fine white stockings. Not a bad way to go, he pondered; at least it was quick.

It was in this year that he came across (and bought, at a high price) certain 'old manuscripts in yellowed ink' from the six-teenth and seventeenth centuries. He would draw on them for his own *Italian Chronicles*. What he found fascinating about them was their sober depiction of violence, their fixation on love and revenge – and, in particular, the theme of imprisonment that ran like a dark thread through them. 'This was the way of life that gave birth to the Raphaels and Michelangelos, even though people naively claim that academies and Schools of Beaux-Arts can produce them [such geniuses] all over again.' He also tried to understand the historical complexities behind these simplicities. 'The Abbess of Castro' begins with an *aperçu* of life in the sixteenth century, when 'brigands' often represented the only real *opposition* to the 'atrocious governments that, in Italy, succeeded the republics of the Middle Ages'. The new tyrant was usually the richest citizen: petty despots like the Medici or the Visconti, paranoid, hypocritical, murderous, were also the ones who built lavish churches and filled them with magnificent paintings. Of course, this was done to 'seduce the lower classes' – but the churches and the paintings were very fine nonetheless. The 'deep hatreds' and 'eternal mistrusts' that arose between tyrants and republicans gave spirit and courage to the Italians of the period, and genius to their artists. There are shades here of the *Third Man* view of art history (war + tyranny produces the Renaissance; brotherly love + democracy produces the cuckoo clock): or of the slightly more nuanced view that civilisation and barbarism go hand in hand.

On 1st September 1835 this lover of dark deeds and acts of passion started wearing glasses and drew a little sketch of himself wearing them, with his dumpy chin and a rather roguish grin. He looked a little like Mr Pickwick. For various reasons – perhaps including his failing eyesight – he now habitually dictated his works rather than writing them. 'Dictating is as boring as the plague, but what else can I do?' One result was to make his work sound even more improvised, or *alla prima*, than before. In November, he examined the *Last Judgement* in the Sistine Chapel with a telescope. The hands in which he was holding the telescope were a little shaky. It was all Michelangelo's fault: on the day before, HB had drunk too much coffee made from a coffee machine which Michelangelo had brought back from London.[93] So, afflicted by a caffeine overdose (and a touch of Stendhal syndrome), and feeling good for nothing – not even for his official duties – he went home, had a fire lit (he suffered increasingly from the cold), and (according to *The Life of Henry Brulard*) carried on writing *The Life of Henry Brulard*. Perhaps this is how we should imagine the writing of his last couple of decades: done *in between* his official activities, scribbled between a couple of boring interviews, jotted down between letters to the ministries back in Paris, dictated between a trip to a local church and dressing for an evening out at the theatre.[94] He wrote *The Life of Henry Brulard* partly as if it were a letter to a friend (albeit one living in 1880). In 1836 he thought he might be suffering from gout in his right hand. He rarely noted his own birthday, but on 2nd December he noted 'Anniversary of Austerlitz'. He started writing his *Memoirs of Napoleon* and sent a draft preface to Mérimée, who complained that the book was disjointed and so allusive that the reader would suspect the author of harbouring republican ideas, in spite of his protestations to the contrary. HB's comments on Napoleon were trite, averred Mérimée: there was no point in trying to prove that Napoleon was a great man when everyone admitted as much; in any case, how could anyone with such a tenuous relation to Napoleon write 'memoirs' of him? HB had, on his own admission, seen Napoleon only four times; they had exchanged words on only three of these occasions; and on one of these Napoleon had uttered nothing but banalities. Why did not HB say, much more honestly, that he had simply lived at court and known the Emperor's ministers?

In September 1837, back in France, HB saw the new train in Saint-Germain-en-Laye, and deplored the 'horrible platitude and coarseness' of Versailles. On 9th September: 'Dance of the bee in Cairo: two lovely *almées* keep crying "Ah! The bee!" and gradually remove all their clothes.' He had been reading a book on modern Egypt: this was about the only thing of interest he had found in it.[95] Unlike many other French writers of the first half of the nineteenth century, he was little drawn to the East – and sceptical about the West. That autumn, in a copy of his *Walks in Rome*, he noted, in a grim pun, the way the New World had copied the old world's crime of slavery: 'The Americans have killed love and joy [*l'amour et la joie*]: they have murdered Mr Lovejoy who had set up a journal to preach the emancipation of the Slaves.'[96] He was what Nietzsche would call 'a good European'. In 1838 he ventured further abroad, on the longest journey he had undertaken since Russia: Bordeaux, the south of France, Grenoble and Switzerland, eastern France and western Germany. In July, suffering from severe gout and hobbling around with a walking stick, swearing every time he stubbed the toes of his left foot on the cobblestones, he was fascinated, not by the Dance of the Bee, but by the Dance of Death that he saw in Strasbourg. He went on to Amsterdam, Rotterdam (where he came across the best strawberries of the year), the Hague, and Brussels.

In October, he corresponded with Delacroix, who said that he could not possibly see people during the day, as he was hard at work in his *atelier*. Three of the painter's works had been turned down by the Institut. HB was indignant: 'The dogs!' Despite this, HB was not really attuned to the latest art; the role of bringing a real critical-empathetic intelligence to contemporary painting and music would soon pass to the man who in an odd way was HB's successor, Charles Baudelaire.

The Charterhouse of Parma

Parma lies outside the route of the ordinary tourist,
and the treasures of its gallery and churches are still unsus-
pected by many.

Estelle M. Hurll

In 1838, during one of his semi-official periods of leave in Paris,
HB noted, 'Opus restarted on 4th November, **the 2d day after my
return of** Rouen.' He was writing or, more often, dictating *The
Charterhouse of Parma*, with its startling evocation of the Battle of
Waterloo, its dream-like escapades, and its obsession with omens,
doomed love, and imprisonment. By 2nd December he was on
page 640. He later regretted dictating the work (in sixty or seventy
sessions), and told Balzac he 'wouldn't do it again' – he had lost
the narrative thread, even though dictating meant that he had
kept his style 'simple'. He finished it on 26th December, and sent
off the six big notebooks to Colomb, who was to forward them
to the publisher: he was very tired, and suffering from neuralgia
in his left leg; but he managed to walk as far as the Bastille. Balzac
wrote him a fan letter on 20th March 1839; he had just read the
'Waterloo' scene in *The Constitutionnel* and it had made him com-
mit the sin of envy – he had been dreaming of something similar
for his own *Scenes of Military Life* and was dazzled by the success
of HB, or rather Frédérick de Stendhal. 'It's like Borgognone and
Vouvermans, Salvator Rosa and Walter Scott,' he enthused. On

11th April, in warm sunlight, on a Paris boulevard, HB met M. de Balzac, who again sang the praises of *The Charterhouse of Parma* ('nothing like it for forty years') but added, 'Cut Parma' – or so HB noted in the margins of a copy of his *Life of Rossini*. For some reason Balzac thought it was a bad idea for the novel to be set in that particular town (HB had chosen it partly for reasons of political prudence). On 28th March, HB read the first printed copy of his novel. In late autumn, he holidayed in Naples with Mérimée. They quarrelled. It was too hot for the plump, sweating HB, and Mérimée was growing commonplace (HB called him 'Academus'[97]); in any case, HB was not a loyal friend: too prickly, beneath his man-of-the-world demeanour, and too easily bored.

Life in Civitavecchia was routine, bureaucratic, dutiful. Like other novelists, however, HB found that the apparently humdrum activities of his day job (he was, after all, responsible for monitoring the activities of French agents throughout the Papal States) could cast odd shafts of illumination on his imaginative life. And, although increasingly prone to an absenteeism that brought down withering remarks from the authorities for whom he was supposedly working (he was off work for 451 days between 17th April 1831 and 1st September 1833, when he went on leave; then away again for 627 days between 8th January 1834 and 11th May 1836, etc.), he was often conscientious[98] – enough to express the hope, at the end of 1833, that he might be awarded the Legion of Honour by Guizot's government. (He wrote to Guizot in May 1834 with a gentle reminder: perhaps, as he lived so far away from Paris, the 'modest little business', i.e. his gong, had been forgotten?[99]) During his periods of absence, this potential subversive was sometimes closely shadowed – by both the Tuscan government and the Holy See, for instance, during his trips to Florence between 1832–4. Thus it was noted by the spy sent to tail him that, on 22nd November 1832, HB entered a patisserie on the Via de' Calzaioli in Florence, and bought 'a quantity of cakes'. This is a man who, these days, would (at least) have had his phone tapped.

In order to make doubly sure that he did not become entirely desk-bound, of which there was admittedly little chance, he also indulged in many trips to Rome. But his view of the capital of the Christian world[100] (although tempered by the realisation that at least it was not Civitavecchia) was ambivalent. Social life was dominated by rich English women – generally 'devout, rigid, and puritanical' – who lived in palaces too big for the Roman princes to maintain. Several crowned heads from Europe (some of them still clinging to their crowns) had taken refuge there: it was like a scene from *Candide*. There were also pretenders, such as the Duke of Bordeaux, a plump, dandified young man with lovely blond hair and a face rather like Louis XVI. He cut a rather effeminate figure when compared to the restless, merry, unpredictable hereditary Grand Duke of Russia, another man biding his time in the Eternal City.

The denizens of the Roman salons, whose freedom to talk was curtailed by the looming presence of the Vatican, were careful what they said, and expressed amusement and sometimes shock at the paradoxes, sallies, dry wit, and general unpredictability of the Consul of Civitavecchia. They did not always realise that he had published, for instance, the *Walks in Rome* which (he claimed) all visitors to Rome now read. The diplomats and monsignors laughed at his jokes, but were aware that he often joked about them when they were not there. Some feared him. He could break out into violent tirades, and vent his frustrations by voicing asinine opinions: one evening, in the *loge* of the French Ambassador, he said that the problems of the current political situation could best be solved by executing all men over fifty (an age on the wrong side of which HB himself now was). Sometimes he became frankly ridiculous, defending, with increasing vehemence, the most absurd paradoxes. One evening, at the Countess Sofia's, he drank too much and was heard to proclaim that a writer should be able to produce comedies and tragedies with equal facility. What a coarse little man he could be, with his chubby cheeks, his ridiculous dyed toupee (he claimed that the snows of Russia were responsible for the baldness of his pate), and those sideburns too, forever advancing down his chin and joining forces in front of his bobbing Adam's apple, and then, a few weeks later, retreating back up to his ears... And what a bore he was on the Renaissance. Anybody would think nobody in the world knew about Michelangelo, or Leonardo, or Correggio, except him. Those who had read his *History of Painting* loved to point out what a farrago it was: fake scholarship, bland generalisations, odd little asides about tyranny (oh, very *political*), the pretence that he had his finger on the pulse of the *cinquecento* merely because street brawls thrilled him and he fancied the local ladies. And as for his habit of crying up Cimarosa and Mozart, the one now an esteemed classic firmly entrenched in the repertoire, the other an entertaining (if slightly lightweight) composer of bubbly divertimenti and somewhat scurrilous operas (*Così fan tutte...*), it just betrayed how much behind the times he was. He was always singing the praises of disinterest, and then moaning about his salary. He would laud the energies of the Italian lower classes, when – as the Count of Stronzino, an Italian liberal, pointed out – these energies were born of despair and vented themselves in random acts of futile violence. Those who knew that the works signed 'Stendhal' had been produced by this jumped-up pen-pusher from dingy, dusty Civitavecchia were sceptical about their value. Their fragmentary nature, the way they played fast-and-loose with the facts, their blandly confident opinionatedness unsupported by any real argument or analysis, their self-reflexive games with epigrams and irony, all reflected too many literary trends of the present day. Soon any hack would narcissistically be copying them; a whole school of epigones (or *beylistas*) would take over culture. And HB sometimes really did go too far. One day, in the house of Ingres (then Director of the Académie française in the Villa Medici), HB claimed that *there was not a single melody in the whole of Beethoven*. Ingres tried to defend the great master, but was met with a torrent of abuse ('German music... too much counterpoint... fusty academic rubbish...').

Ingres eventually turned his back on the unstoppable Consul. 'Please see M. Beyle to the door,' he instructed one of his lackeys. HB shrugged, and departed, never to return to the Villa Medici. Of course, any man of musical honour would surely have acted the same way as Ingres, who not only had impeccable musical taste but was also the finest French painter of the first half of the nineteenth century, and signed some of the most beautiful portraits in the world.[101]

The Charterhouse of Parma moves slowly across the landscapes of France and Italy, through scenes of love and war, to the worst thing of all, a tragically brief life. As HB knew, this death lay somehow at the heart of the work – of his *oeuvre* – and casts a long shadow on 'Kulchur', with all its gibes and gambols. After this death, the protagonists, in rapid succession, lose the will to live. The text, however, lives on, as immensely rich as Count Mosca (or, in *The Red and the Black*, Mathilde de la Mole), but as forlorn as all mere survivors.

All gas and gaiters

I am a barbarian here, since nobody understands me.
Ovid, Tristia

I might as well be in Borneo.
HB in Civitavecchia

'I am imprisoned for stealing half a dozen eggs. Ministers
who rob millions are honoured. Poor Italy!'
A common thief, quoted in Emma Goldman, 'Prisons: a social crime and failure'

The news of the day in mid-May 1839 was the death of Cardinal
Fesch, Archbishop of Lyon – he was the uncle of Napoleon, and
had outlived his tempestuous nephew. Like everything to do
with the Bonaparte family, Fesch's life, and death, were of obses-
sive interest to the heirs of another, more enduring empire than
Napoleon's. But Rome was no longer in Rome, HB decided; it
lacked all energy – except the energy of the brigands and hooli-
gans of the *populus Romanus*, and that of the lovelorn victims of
passions repressed by a Church unsympathetic to Eros. A pretty
nun who lived next door to the Jesuit novitiate hanged herself
for love.[102] HB noted laconically that 'one month later, a secret
execution among the Jesuits' took place. The rumour was going
around that Messieurs de Loyola had quietly got rid of the
young novice involved. It was surprising (but not to the worldly

wise HB) what the passionate adorers of the Sacred Heart of Jesus could get up to.

A little surprisingly, HB ('Only two things make me mad: Popery and lack of freedom') seems to have had a *faible* for Pope Gregory XVI, a man who sometimes decided not to attend religious processions in case he was popenapped by liberals. (For the Jesuits, there were liberals at every street corner; for the liberals, the tentacles of the Society of Jesus reached into every salon.) The Pope had earlier gained a reputation for being over-fond of food and wine, and for being a political reactionary; His Holiness had made a rather good joke, in French: railways were roads to hell – *'chemins de fer'* = *'chemins d'enfer'*. In the Papal States, censorship meant that HB was often denied the news-papers he needed to receive as a Consul (only *Il Diario di Roma* was published in Rome itself; HB soon made sure his own subscription to this worthy journal was cancelled).[103] Gregory's more liberal moments (an encyclical of December 1839 con-demned the slave trade) were overshadowed by his refusal to condemn the reactionary regimes now governing Europe, and the Papal States (which extended eastwards to Rimini and Ancona on the Adriatic, and right up past Bologna to the River Po) were a hotbed of dissent. The Pope often needed to rely on Austrian support to keep the revolutionaries at bay, and his reign saw the usual executions and imprisonments. However, by November 1839, Gregory was suffering from gangrene in his leg, and HB described him as 'kindly' and 'inoffensive', and a lover of natural history who took a lively interest in rare fish. (Despite his gangrene spreading – pus dripped from his nose and seeped from his leg – the Pope, already seventy-six years old, lived on until 1846.)

But an apparently *simpatico* Pope did not prevent justice in the Papal States from being harsh – no harsher than elsewhere, perhaps. Sometimes, Gregory's gaze drifted up to the Greek words (John 21:17) high above the *baldacchino* in St Peter's. In July 1841 (the weather was extraordinarily hot, even for Rome) three murderers – two men and a woman, the latter of whom had killed the family of a clockmaker during the carnival of 1839 – were executed in the Holy City. Their heads were then exposed to the people on stakes (*pals*). The crowd, ever curious, rushed forward to get a closer look; thieves and pickpockets moved in among the distracted spectators; the Papal Guard was jostled and insulted and thereupon charged into the mass, bayonets at the ready. Only the officers' yells stopped the soldiers from firing into the crowd. Over fifty people were wounded. HB commented in a letter to Guizot that 'the lower classes, especially those of Trastevere' were so insolent towards the soldiers that the resentment of the latter was quite understandable. But his odd fascination for the anachronism of the papacy – and for the politics that subtended it[104] – remained. In a short essay on Leo XII, he wrote that a pope could fulfil three roles. He could be 'an insignificant fool, signing papal bulls and visiting churches'. Or he could be 'a real pope', acting in the Church's interest, and thus necessarily 'the most intolerant of men'. The third possibility was 'to turn Rome into a general refuge for all the poor devils banished by their governments – and never has Europe had a more urgent need of such a refuge'. HB was, in certain respects, one such devil finding sanctuary in the Holy City with uncrowned monarchs and other pretenders.

Mare nostrum

The life of the city never lets go.
Wallace Stevens, 'To an Old Philosopher in Rome'

From his position in the main port of Rome, HB could keep under surveillance the sea traffic of the western Mediterranean (Sicily, Capri, Naples, the ports of France and Spain…). Some 288 steamboats per year stopped off in Civitavecchia. HB complained that, due to competition, several French maritime companies failed to observe their timetables, and set sail twenty-four hours earlier or later than scheduled.

He was constrained in the information he sent and received. All letters sent back to France were objects of suspicion to the Papal powers, and the government of the Grand Duke of Tuscany was averse to statistics (it was even unsafe to keep such data in one's home). HB apprised Marshal Soult, then Minister for War, of whatever details he could glean. Soult was the general who had been repeatedly defeated by Wellington in Spain and failed to give Napoleon the support he needed at Waterloo; he had declared himself a royalist when the latter was sent to Elba, a Bonapartist during the Hundred Days, and a royalist after 1820.[105] HB told Soult that he was obliged to keep the traffic passing in and out of Civitavecchia under close observation: in 1839 alone, 16,139 travellers had passed through Civitavecchia, all of them potential subversives requiring monitoring – there were

Miguelists, Carlists, and assorted other plotters, not all of them from the Iberian peninsula. 'The Consulate needs to keep up with everything that happens, and to inform the King's Embassy in Rome and often the Embassy in Naples too.' For all these reasons HB requested a rise in his salary (or at least drafted the letter).

In May 1840 he was writing to Adolphe Thiers, Foreign Minister (for a while) under Louis-Philippe,[106] to inform him, not of an outbreak of plague or cholera (keeping tabs on this latter, terrifying disease was one of HB's duties[107]), but of a more humdrum business. The French Consul told Thiers that French cod was unlikely to obtain favour in the Roman States unless it was salted with alum or a similar product to preserve it from the heat of the summer. Otherwise the Romans would continue to eat English cod – less tasty, but easier to preserve, since it *was* packed in alum. Later, HB wrote to the Foreign Minister, this time Guizot, to give him details of the salt and tobacco trade in Italy, of the importing of coals from Newcastle (expensive: thirty-five to forty francs per ton), and of the condition of coral fishing off the coasts of the Papal States (the coral found in the seas around Civitavecchia was particularly attractive, redder than that found off Africa or Sardinia).

In short, HB corresponded with some of the most significant figures in nineteenth-century politics about some of the most momentous issues of the day. And he was forced, *ex officio* (and not only *ex officio*) to be aware of the daily conditions of life for the poorest people in the states of the Pope: he wrote of how the workers involved in the extraction of *pozzolana* (used in cement) benefited little from their toils in the quarries of San Paolo, one league away from Rome, since the loading and unloading were done on the cheap by the convicts of Civitavecchia.

HB also took an interest in events back in France. During a stay in Paris (officially sick leave) in December 1841 (it was raining every day, but quite warm) he went to see the trial of Quenisset, who had made an attempt on the lives of the Dukes of Orléans, Nemours and Aumale on 13th September. 'The rascal has a great deal of logic to him,' he commented. In *Memoirs of an Egotist* he claimed that he himself had thought seriously of murdering Louis XVIII. (Not for nothing would Mérimée later refer to him as a 'colleague of the Brutuses, etc.'.) But then, at that time (in the 1820s) he had been half-crazed by disappointed love for Metilde. He knew that such incriminating evidence would not pose any danger for him; his *Memoirs*, with their 'I- planned-to-kill-Louis-XVIII' confession, would be published posthumously. It would be so amusing when they finally came out and were exhibited in the windows of the Palais-Royal bookstores, in 1860! But by that date, he added maliciously, the Palais-Royal might not be called the Palais-*Royal*.[108]

Crates full of books and bones

The fetishist is artful…
Freud

HB also attended a canonisation presided over by Gregory XVI. St Peter's was filled with a throng of handsome young bishops in their finest attire. HB gazed at them in admiration – he often succumbed to the sheer spectacle of life in the Vatican: the brilliant apparel, the glorious music, the thrillingly disembodied voice of the castrati, the curling clouds of incense. Never had such gorgeous flowers arrayed the chains of the people! (Or *were they really chains?*) Still, HB's anti-clericalism was too deeply implanted for him entirely to lose his head over any theocratic *bella figura* – though, in a curious will of May 1834, he did write as if he had been tempted by Protestantism, 'I die in the bosom of the Reformed Church and desire to be interred near M. Shelley, an Englishman, near the Pyramid of Cestius (Rome).' Perhaps he liked the shade offered by the lovely trees of the little Protestant cemetery.[109]

After the canonisation in question, the Pope later sent the French Consul a crate full of relics of the new saints, to be forwarded to the President of the Propagation of the Faith in Lyon. One of the saints canonised in 1839 was the beautiful and pious Veronica Giuliani, a stigmatic and mystic who – like many mystics – was endowed with considerable practical sense. As

Abbess of the Poor Clares' convent in Città di Castello, Umbria, she had installed an impressive plumbing system.

Crates of bones left Rome; crates of books came in, and were closely monitored. HB's own crates from France were on at least one occasion inspected by the Papal authorities, despite the hypocritical protestations of his chancellor, Lysimaque Tavernier (HB was away in Paris at the time). Lysimaque Caftangi-Oglou Tavernier was an interesting man, of Greek-French origin; whether his boss HB was there or not, he tended to assume many of the functions of a consul; he was one of the driven, somewhat demonic copyist-secretaries so important in nineteenth-century culture, though he also took the initiative in ways that made HB amused and sometimes angry. 'You can call yourself Vice-Consul if you like,' he noted to Lysimaque, 'but not in writing. You're just a chancellor, and you sign, "P.p. Monsieur le Consul, who is ill".' And, after several rows in which Lysimaque had risen above his station, HB wrote that his chancellor was 'black-hearted, wicked, a dreamer, a wretch'. HB even on one occasion accepted his tearful resignation, only to reinstate him, albeit with reluctance. Behind a façade of obsequious loyalty to HB, Tavernier seems to have been angling for the latter's own job; to this end, he obtained French nationality, and wrote to Paris to complain about his master's absenteeism.[110]

On the occasion of HB's crates arriving in Civitavecchia, Tavernier insisted a little bit too much that the diplomatic forms be respected, and thus (perhaps deliberately) heightened the authorities' interest in the contents. There was an agreement that such packages had something of the status of diplomatic bags; but at times of suspicion (in practice, at any time), the Pope's police could override this convention. They opened them, and found a variety of books, of which they drew up an inventory.

Some of the books were forbidden in papal domains: these they marked with a cross. These included a life of Pius V; Stendhal's *Rome, Naples and Florence in 1817*; and works by Montesquieu, Condorcet, Voltaire, Montaigne, Helvétius, Machiavelli, and

Bayle.[111] Two works (a life of Pope Alexander VI and his son, and *Les Amours du chevalier de Faublas* by Louvet de Couvray) were especially forbidden ('+++'). Others were 'censurable': Stendhal's *On Love*, and his *The Red and the Black* and *Walks in Rome*; a louche and risqué tale of forbidden love in the seventeenth century by Madame de Lafayette called *The Princess of Cleves* (a 'divine' work, thought HB, who preferred its psychological analysis to Walter Scott's local colour); and the *Memorial of Saint-Helena*. One further category of books (or to-be-books) was deemed merely 'suspect': it included a number of dubious memoirs in French and Italian, and some of HB's manuscript works (*Lucien Leuwen*, *Memoirs of a Tourist*). The Count of La Tour-Maubourg protested in the strongest terms to Cardinal Lambruschini, Secretary of State at the Vatican: how dare the papal police treat a Consul of France as a suspect? Lambruschini – a rather conservative Secretary of State, who viewed gaslights as an invention of the Devil – wrote a half-hearted apology, but claimed that it was Tavernier's odd behaviour that had first aroused suspicion. Either way, as a note in the secret archives of the Vatican shows, HB (a *persona* never quite *grata* wherever he went) was duly placed under the surveillance of the *carabinieri pontifici* in October.

In 1840, on New Year's Day, HB fell into his fire while correcting his last, unfinished, enigmatic novel *Lamiel*, in which an enticing young woman takes the initiative for her own sexual education, but is initially somewhat disappointed ('Is that all it is?'). '**Last Romance**' he wrote at this time; his last love seems to have been a woman he called 'Earline', probably the Countess Cini.[112] He thought of her (but 'not tragically') in the Forum of Rome, and went to a ball in the great Colonna Palace: crowned (or once-crowned) heads were present, but he had eyes only for Earline; there she stood, in the passage just left of the door. Rome, romance... This was the time of last times (declining into uncomfortable, grouchy late middle age, he decided to give 'Earline' a copy of Walter Scott's *Old Mortality*). There was a last time he hummed a tune from *Il Matrimonio segreto*, a last time he felt the cold creeping up his leg, a last time he rolled, with a grunt and a sigh, off a woman, a last time he admired the cirrus clouds in the autumn skies over Castel Sant'Angelo, a last time he thought of the dark eyes of beloved, disdainful Metilde, long since dead and buried.

It was in April, that month of fools, that HB composed his 'Privileges'. This marvellous document is a kind of Faustian pact, but this time with **God** rather than His opposite number; and it seems to be a one-way deal, in that the 'privileges' granted by the Deity do not appear to require anything in return.[113] **God** gave HB the right not to suffer from any serious pain until advanced old age, when he would die, not painfully, but by apoplexy. His *mentula*[114] would be as hard and reliable as an index finger. He would enjoy the love of women, at times and places indicated; he would play whist, billiards, chess, and other games perfectly well; he would be able to change into the animal of his choice four times per year. Anyone who tried to murder him would be afflicted by acute cholera (but only for a week; the beneficiary of the Privileges was a humane fellow – he was allowed to kill ten human beings per year, but *only so long as he had not spoken to them*). Little flags would usefully indicate the site of buried treasure, or the lairs of game animals to be hunted. If he prayed in due form for his food, a plate of spinach (etc.) would be served to him. At the times and places appointed, he would be able to lessen the sufferings of sentient beings around him. He would never be more unhappy than he had been from 1st August 1839 to 1st April 1840. He would read people's minds, he would be happy with the modest (but very sufficient) sum of sixty francs per day. In this way, the new Beylusalem would come down from the heavens, arrayed like a bride to the banquet.

In May 1840 he again read Winckelmann (he had earlier called him 'Winckelmann, first baron of Steindhal [*sic*!]') but the latter was 'a declaimer without ideas'. But HB hated having to study; reviews were written by pedants, foreign books were ruined by the 'boundless stupidity' of translators. He was most of all preoccupied by the question of style as he tried to 'polish' *The Charterhouse of Parma*, in reaction to Balzac's critiques. In a letter to Balzac (he drafted three versions, the first of which he rejected as being 'frightfully egotistic': we do not have the one he finally sent), HB had defended his novel against the negative remarks the younger writer had made in an otherwise astute and positive review. He had not expected to be read before 1880... he had already, on what he took to be Balzac's advice, reduced the first fifty-four pages to a mere four or five... he would add a new episode in which Rassi and Co. would appear at the Opera in Paris, sent there by Ranuce-Ernest to spy things out after Waterloo... But he was still anxious to avoid the 'overblown' quality that he so much hated among his contemporaries, especially Mme de Staël and Chateaubriand,[115] and the 'falsehoods' that he found in Rousseau or George Sand. He didn't want ('Pardon the vulgar word', he told Balzac) to 'wank off' the reader's soul. True, his novel would be more successful if George Sand translated it into French – but then it would be twice as long. When tempted to add more colour or atmosphere, to be a bit more fashionable, to 'put on yellow gloves', as he put it, he resisted. To get the tone of the *Charterhouse* right, he had occasionally read a few pages of the *Code civil*.[116]

The Charterhouse of Parma, unlike the Farnese Tower, really exists, and is well worth visiting. You can take a bus from Parma bus station; but the bus companies there seem to have taken to heart Nietzsche's dictum 'I love uncertainty about the future', and a bus with number sixteen on its front may travel along a variety of routes to a variety of destinations. Despite the recommendations of some *impiegati,* it is best to avoid bus number seven (marked '*Carcere*'[117]). In fact, it is best to avoid the buses altogether and walk out to the Charterhouse; the route takes you through some of Parma's pretty suburbs, and – if you set out early in the morning – you will be rewarded by the sight of the campanile of the Charterhouse looming dreamily in the mist against the rising sun. On arrival, you will discover that the famous Charterhouse of Parma is now a police training school. One of the elegantly uniformed staff will be happy to show you round the beautiful church and the cloisters, with their *cellae* for the individual Carthusians, where Fabrice spent his last year. No true Stendhalian should miss out on this experience. Admittedly, some have claimed that the Charterhouse HB had in mind was actually the so-called 'Certosa di Paradigna', a quite different building, a photograph of which is (for some strange reason) now often used on the cover of Italian translations of HB's great novel. But the building at Paradigna was never a Charterhouse, belonging as it did to the Cistercian order; and those who have acquired blistered feet on the long, hot walk out to the *real* Charterhouse of Parma can rest assured that they are authentic Stendhalian pilgrims, paying homage to the place where Fabrice sought solace.

HB gradually abandoned the attempt to improve the *Charterhouse* and went shooting instead (one autumn day he shot seven larks, '**the first time in my life, I suppose**').

In December 1840, the remains of Napoleon were brought back to France from St Helena and there was considerable debate on the kind of monument to be raised to the mighty Emperor. HB had his own ideas. Maybe a brick copy of the temple at Paestum (the 'most beautiful thing in Italy') could be erected at Saint-Cloud? But it *must not be embellished by MM. the Members of the French Academy.* Maybe a round tower, 150 feet high and 100 feet in diameter, like the Castel Sant'Angelo (originally the tomb of Hadrian) in Rome? Napoleon, of course, eventually got the monument he so richly deserved, in a revamped Invalides.

HB was bored in Rome, it was cold and rainy, and, since it was the penitential season of Advent, the possibilities for entertainment were limited. His diary for 1840 ends with a string of '**Dates of his life**', '**Life**', '**His life**' (one of these empty lists goes: 1833–4, 1833, 1812, 1840, 1833, 1830: the only thing he could remember about his trip to Florence in 1833–4 was the eclipse of the moon).

In 1841, he noted 'Earline fades **from his soul**' (but he started contemplating a novel 'about' her). He started to mellow towards that 'despot' Louis XIV, who 'had a poetic soul which the Duke de Saint-Simon never understood'. In February, one visit to his doctor produced a prescription for *nux vomica* and belladonna; another added aconite, and a further one an enema with half a glass of cold water morning and evening. HB really wanted to be bled: he knew he had high blood pressure. His mood was now autumnal; he had written that art was a *'promesse de bonheur'* or promise of happiness, a formula approved by Nietzsche; but sometimes the happiness of art seemed to consist entirely of art itself, and its handmaid, memory.

On 16th February he noted, 'Douyoupre ferhavinghadth reewom enorhav ingwrit tenthisvelno?' (in the original, *'Aimetumie uxavoireut roisfem mesoua voirfa itcemanro?'*). In April he had an attack of apoplexy, a brush with the void – the most disagreeable aspect of which was 'all the stupid ideas people put into our heads at the age of three'. After all, you might as well die in the street as anywhere else ('so long as you don't do it on purpose'). Observing himself, as ever, he noted the symptoms that had preceded the attack: six months of horrible migraines, incipient aphasia (he would suddenly forget all his French: 'I can no longer say "Give me a glass of water"'). Inspecting the work produced by the students at the Académie de France he almost suffocated, and his face went crimson: but this may have been brought on as much by the 'total dullness' of the work on exhibition as by apoplexy. In July he remarked that he had suffered from '**four months of firodea**' (fear of… a word he preferred not to complete: his Anglo-Beylish term resembles the name of a minor Roman deity, Firodea).[118] His love of ciphers and cryptograms continued to amuse and irritate his friends. This man, so adept at disguising himself from himself and his intimates, often gave himself away when discretion was part of his official duties. HB once sent a ciphered letter to M. de Broglie, French Minister of Foreign Affairs, and absent-mindedly (though, with HB, who knows?) included the key to the code in the same envelope. The Minister was obliged to urge more caution.

In October, HB took leave of absence and handed over the Consulate in Civitavecchia to Lysimaque Tavernier before departing for France. He would never see Italy again.

18th January 1842 (he was in Paris): 'I have no reputation in 1842.' There is one real reason for this: 'Literary life as it exists in 1840 is a wretched life. It awakens the most contemptible instincts in our nature, those that are the most productive of petty unhappiness.' (Signed:) H. BEYLE. Contemporaries worried at how much he had changed. Gone were the days, back in the 1820s, when he had enthralled and alarmed the salons of Paris with his aggressive *boutades*, his fierce paradoxes, his subversive jokes; when the man of letters Etienne-Jean Delécluze had felt so guilty at lending an ear to HB's tirades against de Maistre, the religious party, the priests, and even God that he had felt obliged to confess his tarrying with the enemy to his parish priest. (The priest absolved him; Delécluze, unable to resist temptation, soon slunk guiltily back to the salons to get another dose of HB's diabolical *esprit*.) Now HB's mind wandered, his sallies were blunt, his wit uncertain, he was now much *nicer* – an alarming sign.

Salve, Firodea Magna

I probably won't leave much behind except for a few books.
HB

During his stay in France, HB went hunting in the beautiful
forests of Compiègne, annoyed only by the fact that he was
obliged to make conversation with his fellow hunters (in the
solitudes of Civitavecchia he had been able to combine shooting
with his usual reveries). He planned an excursion to Versailles,
and took a walk to the Bastille. On 22nd March 1842 he wrote,
'**Yesterday**, 15.' This was probably the number of pages dictated
or written of his latest story, 'Suora Scolastica'. It was his last
diary entry. That evening, **God**, freely complying with article
one of the 'Privileges of 10th April 1840', struck him down,
gently, with apoplexy, in the street. HB was taken to his rooms,
but did not regain consciousness. He was fifty-nine years and
three months old.

'Suora Scolastica' is a baroque tale set in mid eighteenth-
century Naples. Rosalinde, the prince's daughter, is loved by
the poor nobleman Gennarino. She is sent to a convent by her
father; the lovers still contrive to meet, but are discovered by
the Abbess. Gennarino is arrested; Rosalinde is condemned to
perpetual imprisonment in the *souterrains* of the convent. You
can almost hear the music (Donizetti? Early Verdi?). But HB
himself had no idea how his story was going to end.

The news of his death roused mild interest in the newspapers (there were brief notices of the death of 'M. Bayle', 'Frédéric Stendhal', and even 'Bayle-Frédéric Styndall', author of 'several esteemed books'). His friends were saddened; ex-colleagues such as Tavernier saw their chance (though when Tavernier eventually was appointed to a consulate, it was in Baghdad); many in the Papal States were relieved. Cardinal Lambruschini was informed that HB had, 'under the false name of Frédéric Stendhal', vilified the grave doctrines of the Church; it was pitiful to see the way that he had been punished by 'Divine justice'. It could at least be hoped that the next consul would not propagate 'bad books' among the inhabitants of the Pope's domains.

The faithful Colomb started on the task of gathering manuscripts and souvenirs. HB had left many effects, including portraits of women friends (Mme Pasta, Mme Lafarge) and Napoleon, together with an umbrella in very poor shape[119] and a map of the French Empire. Articles about HB started appearing; those who had known HB realised how little they had known him, or rather, how differently he had appeared to every one of them. Each memoir-writer started indignantly criticising the others. The hunt for sources (not always a form of the hunt for happiness) began in earnest. Balzac, convinced (despite HB's own demurrals) that Christine Trivulzio, Princess of Belgiojoso, was the origin of some characteristics of Sanseverina in the *Charterhouse*, sent her a copy of the novel. She replied rather tartly that, though she had greatly enjoyed the novel, she did not recognise any of the alleged portraits in it. 'No Italian woman is as active as the Duchess [Sanseverina], and no Italian man is as immobile as the Count [Mosca]. Movement and rest succeed each other at shorter intervals among us [Italians]. We are soon wearied by the one; we are soon bored by the other; we have no staying power.' Then she invited Balzac to attend a spiritualist séance.

It slowly dawned on HB's readers that, even in his non-fiction works, many of his characters – such as those he had used to guide the reader along his *Walks in Rome* – were actually fictitious![120] They started gathering his letters ('interesting… crazy…'), his scattered texts, his manuscripts, his brochures and pamphlets. They were dismayed to see how much was left in an unfinished state. One and a half hundredweight of manuscripts! What on earth to do with them? It was a shame to select (though Crozet and Balzac suggested a judicious selection), and impossible to expect people to read everything (though Colomb inclined to a more 'completist' point of view). Louis Crozet pointed out to Colomb that HB had been just too witty in every line he wrote; it was wearying to read him for too long. His subtle analyses of the human mind were *so* last century! He was out of date, he was too little of a specialist, he was too much of a materialist (and in the 1840s, a man who showed such hatred for the religious spirit would not be welcome). Mérimée continued to recommend that HB's work be shorn of its 'facetious' political allusions; for all his 'aristocratic' bearing, our friend's stories betrayed a definite tinge of socialism – which he would never have shown if he had lived in 1851. He would lose readers if his 'outbursts against society' were to be published now.

In any case, his horrible handwriting meant that his words had to be guessed at rather than read. Some said that everything he wrote was already in code; his employees had sometimes needed to attach a fair copy to the impenetrable official letters he penned during his Consulate. He once claimed, in a letter of 4th November 1834, that he wrote badly on purpose, to prevent any 'indiscreet person' from reading into his soul. His love of mystification also handed him over to the diligent work of his editors. Without their efforts, half the fun in reading HB would be lost: we would not know what a spin he put on contemporary realities unless we had some inkling of what those realities involved. HB can also count scholars such as Victor del Litto, Philippe Berthier and Michel Crouzet as his honorary pseudonyms.

HB's *Memoirs of an Egotist*[121] bear on their title page the words, 'Not to be published until at least ten years after my departure, out of *délicatesse* for the people named, even though two thirds of them are now dead.' The Preface (signed, for once, 'H. Beyle') bequeaths the manuscript to Abraham Constantin of Geneva, a fine Swiss painter and draughtsman,[122] with instructions that it would be a good idea if some identities could be changed. In fact, concludes HB, 'I'd really like *all* the names to be changed': the real ones could always be reinserted if his 'chatterings' were republished fifty years after his death. For instance, for the 'Mme Doligny and Mme Berthois' in his text, we can read 'Mme Durand and Mme Delpierre'. Except that the last two names are themselves fictitious. The *real* names of the women involved were...

But an edition was assembled; and, slowly, HB was turned into Stendhal.

Stendhal viewed by his contemporaries

'Personally, I'm picking a lottery ticket; the main prize comes down to being read in 1935.'
Stendhal

'But the boy's as ignorant as a carp!'
Pierre Daru, on discovering that his cousin had written a History of Painting in Italy

'Detestable... You write like a porter.'
Victor Jacquemont, HB's friend, to HB

'*C'est bien.*'
Napoleon, on learning of HB's conscientious service as auditeur in Brunswick

'Can't he write like everyone else?... He needs to be clearer, to follow the rules... not serious enough... careless... a continual affectation of originality, pretending to express strange and singular ideas... his language is as unintelligible as his character is indecipherable... desperately mediocre... boring... irreligious... immoral... frivolous... Stendhal's irony often has all the grace of a dancing elephant...'
Various reviewers

'One of the most distinguished and original intelligences of the period... the only man whose hand Diderot might nowadays have been glad to shake...'
Another reviewer

'So, poor Beyle has died. He loved me as much as any man who eats can love. He died of apoplexy after leaving his table, like the man of wit he had been, – and his hand on the pocket of his waistcoat, for fear someone might swipe his watch. It was a bit too late to take such precautions now!

'He was a selfish old bachelor, small, ugly, foul-mouthed [*ordurier*], dozy, half-blind, paradoxical, a man of forced enthusiasm [*enthousiaste à froid*], nasty behind your back and mealy-mouthed to your face.

'But one of the most ingenious and truest novelists we have ever had.

'I'll lend you *The Charterhouse of Parma*, you'll have time to read it. Goodnight!'
Paul-Emile Fargues to Paul Gavarni, midnight, 23rd March 1842, just after HB's death

'Yesterday, I read in bed the first volume of *The Red and the Black*, by Stindahl [sic]. It strikes me as being the work of a distinguished mind, a mind of great delicacy. The style is French. But *is* that style, real style, that old style we no longer find these days?'
Gustave Flaubert in 1845

'I know *The Red and the Black*, and find it badly written and incomprehensible, both its characters and the intentions behind it.'
Gustave Flaubert in 1852

'Charming.'
George Sand on The Charterhouse of Parma

'He made a great effort to appear wicked, but he wasn't such a bad man at heart.'
George Sand on HB

'That mixture of dandy, officer, artist, man of the world, original thinker, humorist, tourist, eccentric and ironist which comprised the fabulous Chimera who answered to the name of Beyle…'
Barbey d'Aurevilly

'Beyle had odd eccentricities of character; they hampered the natural seduction that his company afforded; conversation with him was too often strewn with little asperities that you noticed only when they suddenly struck you, and took away some of the indescribable charm that it would otherwise have had.'
Romain Colomb

'He was one of the most remarkable minds of our age; but he did not take enough care of the *form*, he wrote as the birds sing […] We were going to prune down *The Charterhouse of Parma,* and a second edition would have made it a complete, irreproachable work of art. Still, it's a marvellous book, the book of distinguished minds.'
Balzac

'I occasionally praise Stendhal as a profound psychologist – and yet I have come across professors at German universities who have asked me to spell his name.'
'Might I even perhaps be jealous of Stendhal? He pinched the best atheist joke that I myself might have made: "God's only excuse is that he doesn't exist."'
Nietzsche

'I am in his debt more than any other's. I owe my knowledge of war to him. Reread his account of the battle of Waterloo in *The Charterhouse of Parma*. Who, until then, had described war in such terms, that is, the way it really seems?'
Tolstoy, in 1901

'He is the father of us all.'
Zola

'What a description of passion!'
James Joyce, on The Red and the Black

'That pet of all those who like their French plain... Stendhal's clichés... Worthless... overrated... paltry.'
Nabokov

He lived among 'women of flesh and blood'; he 'does not limit himself to describing his heroines as a function of his heroes: he gives them a destiny of their own'
Simone de Beauvoir, on Stendhal

'He could never make up his mind whether he wanted to be Spinoza or Stendhal.'
Simone de Beauvoir, on Sartre

'Stendhal's dictum about art's *promesse de bonheur* implies that art owes something to empirical life, namely the Utopian content which is foreshadowed by art. [...]
If art wishes to be faithful to that *promesse*, it must have to break it, for any happiness that we may gain in, or in relation to, the existing world is vicarious and false.'
Adorno

Postscript: the Charterhouse

Always present on the young HB's horizon, not far from Grenoble, and close to the paradisiacal estate of Les Échelles where he spent so many happy hours, loomed the GREAT CHARTERHOUSE, situated in an isolated valley at the foot of the Grand Som (some 2,000 metres high), with the Col de la Ruchère to the north and the river Guiers to the south. In his *Memoirs of a Tourist*, HB notes how, in the countryside nearby, 'The peasant girls, in their finest attire, sell little bundles of cherries, and wonderful strawberries gathered from the woods near the Grande Chartreuse.' In the same work he recalls (or invents) a visit he made to the Grande Chartreuse with some fellow tourists. The presence of ladies caused some consternation among the Carthusians. The party spent a night in the monastery – he claims – and he himself attended mass in the gloomy chapel, in the middle of a violent thunderstorm: a scene worthy of the gothic novels from which he had no doubt taken it.

Here, in 1084, Saint Bruno – led by the Bishop of Grenoble – started, with the help of his six companions, to build a monastery where they could worship God in solitude. They took the name of the contemplative order they founded (the Carthusians) from the Latin name of the locality (Carthusia).

The original buildings have largely disappeared, but the Chartreuse still exists, and some at least of its original solitude has been preserved. It is known to the outside world largely through the green liqueur made by the monks, a poem by Matthew Arnold, and a fine film, *Into Great Silence*, which met with acclaim on its release in 2005. Traffic is kept away from the monastic buildings: only birds are allowed to fly through the otherwise empty skies above. The monks spend most of their time alone, except when they assemble for prayers or manual labour; they lead a life of prayer, silence, and austerity, far from the noise of the world. They are sheltered by the high mountains which stretch out towards the Alps, and Italy.

Victorine Bigillion, one of HB's first boyhood loves, perhaps (his feelings for her were uncertain), suffered a cruel destiny; this fresh, buxom country girl was early afflicted by mental instability, and her feelings for HB may have contributed to aggravating her condition. She was hidden away in a *cella* of the Grande Chartreuse and, despite periods of remission, never fully recovered.

There was a family tradition that one of her distant ancestors had welcomed Bruno to the future site of the Grande Chartreuse in 1084, when Gregory VII was Pope in Rome and Henry IV wore the Iron Crown of Lombardy.[123]

Notes

1. All published by Hesperus Press.
2. 'Make loads of money!'
3. This is written in the autumn of 2008.
4. In *The Red and the Black* we read that the motto of the inhabitants of Verrières was 'TO BRING IN MONEY'. But, he points out, Verrières is an imaginary place.
5. His nickname apparently comes from the bear found on his coat of arms (as on those of Saxony-Anhalt even today), rather than from any bear-like traits he may have possessed. See Carlyle, *Frederick the Great*.
6. See the article in Wikipedia for further details. The town's official website is http://www.stendal.de/.
7. Another theory has it that 'Stendhal' has nothing at all to do with Stendal but is an anagram of 'Shetland', a place much admired by the notorious French hoaxer Georges Perec, who first mooted this theory. It is unclear whether Beyle ever visited the Shetland Islands; he certainly got as far north as Newcastle.
8. Actually, Barcelona.
9. This was quite false. The late eighteenth century saw opera start to flourish in the Land of the Free: in particular, unlike in the Old World, women were active in the operatic scene both as librettists (Ann Julia Hatton, Susanna Rowson) and as composers (Alexandra Reinagle – her *Slaves of Algiers, or A Struggle for Freedom* premiered in 1794).
10. This particular pseudonym was in fact used by Beyle in an article commenting on the use of the English word 'puff' meaning 'to praise the merits of'. He suggested creating a French verb, *'poffer'*, meaning 'to praise brazenly and excessively'. He loathed having to do this directly – it was part of the world of cliques and cabals that he thought had taken over the administration of cultural goods in France – but puffed his own work in more discreet ways, often reviewing (pseudonymously) his own (pseudonymous) works.
11. So he was not actually the Universal Author responsible for producing all of modern French literature – a figure found in Georges Perec's *The Winter Journey*.
12. He joked that he was fully in touch with his feminine side, but preferred being in touch with the feminine side of others, especially women.
13. He had not. This was the birth date of his older brother, who had survived for only a few days, and whose tenuous identity he occasionally adopted.
14. Cf. biographers who call Flaubert 'Gustave' because they have read his private letters.

15. The name means 'The Ladders'.

16. Metilde, q.v. *infra*.

17. His odd *insouciance* about ages and dates should not be taken as indifference; he simply had his own calendar. He remembered the death date of his mother well enough when, years later, he began composing his autobiographical *Life of Henry Brulard* on the forty-fifth anniversary of her death, 23rd November 1835.

18. Years later he was impressed at the way Dante was revered by the subversive *carbonari* of Lombardy. Even liberals started to look askance at anyone who loved Dante too much. Dante was almost a *Jacobin*!

19. This was the nineteenth century – so no allusion to similar quarrels *de nos jours*.

20. Jean-Pierre Claris de Florian (1755–94) was a writer of pastoral verse who died in the gaols of the French Revolution: the catch-lines of some of his fables have become proverbial ('*Pour vivre heureux, vivons cachés*': 'To live happy, let us live hidden').

21. Like Beethoven, HB could say, 'I love trees more than I love human beings.' His whole politics was dictated by a love of trees. He praised Napoleon for wakening Italy from its torpor, but even more for planting trees along the roads of Bologna, Naples, and Milan. At the Restoration, HB mocked the citizens of Grenoble for the abhorrent zeal with which they destroyed 'four poplars planted in honour of the Army of Italy as it passed through the town'. They were even so cowardly as to carry out this act of arboricide *under cover of night*. He thought that the English love of trees made them akin to Michelangelo; English trees were 'sublime', especially their 'venerable oaks', several of which had been around at the time of William the Conqueror. Karl Marx too loved trees, especially cherry trees, which gave him a comforting feeling of 'sensuous certainty' (see *The German Ideology*, where he praises Feuerbach for similar insights – while pointing out that cherry trees, just like observations about cherry trees, grow only in determinate historico-political circumstances).

22. From his youth onwards, HB was surrounded by people who thought him ugly, but: 1) charming, 2) ugly like Socrates, i.e. with an *inner beauty*, 3) witty. Even the critic Sainte-Beuve thought that the eloquent sparkle in his eyes compensated for his Kalmuk nose (as if this were a defect!). Sartre identified with HB for all these reasons.

23. Still, his native city would later honour its most celebrated writer: the University of Grenoble-III is named after Stendhal. Grenoble is renowned for its skiing opportunities and its hi-tech industries; unfortunately, it is also known for its drug-trafficking, and for endemic gang warfare which reminds some people of scenes from the perpetually violent city-states of the Italian Renaissance. Varces-Grenoble prison, set in the beautiful hilly woodlands just outside the city, is notorious for its overcrowded and insanitary conditions.

24. 'Cela' = 'that', but also 'he concealed'. 'Cella' = 'cella', a storeroom or chamber, or the cell of a monastic institution. The mistake stuck in HB's mind: Julien Sorel makes the same slip in *The Red and the Black* and ends up in a prison cell.

25. In the *Life of Rossini* he recalls a sweet-tempered, polite man in Brescia who would register his pleasure at a musical concert by taking off his shoes without even noticing; at a really 'sublime' passage, he would throw them over his shoulder into the audience.

26. Words in bold are in Anglo-Beylish in the original. HB often resorted to this dialect of English in his diaries and letters. It is not to be confused with 'franglais', nor with Gallo-Betjemanesque ('Cher M'lle, J'ai correcté les typescripts. A la meme temps j'ai made a list of suitable illustrations qui je suis keeping pour aide memoire quand nous come to review le whole libre', etc.).

27. See for instance a marginal note HB scribbled, on the last day of 1834, in his copy of *Lucien Leuwen*: 'This is called not giving a damn about a bloody thing. **O happy State!**'

28. For full details of the Emperor's day-by-day, hour-by-hour schedule, see the *Itinéraire de Napoléon Bonaparte* (1947), especially p. 223.

29. Back in the Dauphiné.

30. The post of Auditeur du Conseil d'État was created by Napoleon in 1803. The appointees were basically young men who assisted ministers of state; their reward, if they were good, was to attend sessions of the Conseil d'État where they would *see Napoleon in person*.

31. HB's work is full of comparisons such as this. Another was: 'Mozart was the Walter Scott of music', since they were both good at 'description'. All the things he loved and admired had to resemble each other. His code-name for Napoleon was 'Milan': the admired Emperor and the adored city had to be, on some deep level, identical.

32. Years later, the ageing *Geheimrat* Goethe praised the psychological acumen of HB in *The Red and the Black*, but thought HB's women were rather idealised. Goethe had earlier been amused to discover that HB had plagiarised his work in his writings on Rome. HB, without knowing Goethe's work well, was a great admirer of at least *this* German.

33. During his time in Germany, HB preferred to study English rather than learn German.

34. She was the daughter of a Prussian general before becoming ruler of All The Russias.

35. Cf. his reaction to a similar visitors' book at the summit of Mount Vesuvius.

36. He wrote this terrifying cannonade into the 'Dona nobis pacem' of the *Missa Solemnis*.

37. By Goldsmith, actually.

38. In *The Life of Henry Brulard* he claims on the first page that he had been there; a few pages later he informs us that he was just boasting.

39. Admittedly, this letter is signed 'L.-A. Bohaire, Bookseller'. But it is in HB's handwriting.

40. This fine example of imperial kitsch, known as the 'Table d'Austerlitz ou des Maréchaux' (it seems that HB was not being ironic in his praise of it), designed by the fine draughtsman Charles Percier and decorated by Jean-Baptiste Isabey, can be seen in the collection at Rueil-Malmaison.

41. 'He lived, he wrote, he loved' – an epitaph he invented for himself.

42. Of course, it depends on the newspaper. In 1827, HB complained in his diary, in the middle of a reflection on 'style', 'The ear is spoiled by reading the newspapers: *every morning* it takes up a whole hour.' But this implies that he did read them – with an eye always open for anecdotes to transfer into his novels.

43. In Hobbes's wonderful definition, laughter is 'sudden glory'.

44. It was Philippe Pinel who freed the women in the asylum-prison of La Salpêtrière from their chains. HB had read Pinel's work on madness in 1806.

45. Mlle de Lespinasse was a brilliant eighteenth-century salon hostess and friend of D'Alembert; her passionate love affairs (her love for the Count de Guibert, who married another woman, hastened her collapse and death) are recounted in her letters.

46. The unpopular Minister Giuseppe Prina was beaten to death by umbrellas nearby, in April 1814.

47. *The Stendhal Syndrome* is a 1996 film by Dario Argento, starring his daughter, the lovely Asia. It is an excellent introduction to Stendhal's world, with its Renaissance art, violence, sensuality, and enigmatic sense of redemption.

48. 'The waters bare up the ark' – Genesis 7:17.

49. There will never come a fourth. See *Ivan the Terrible*, etc.

50. And just as it did at the end of the twentieth century.

51. And, of course, Pierre Bezuhov.

52. Most likely the *Paul et Virginie* of Bernardin de Saint-Pierre, in the excellent English translation (*The Shipwreck*) by Ann Lemoine (1800).

53. As we have seen, HB did indeed have an older brother, Marie-Henri, who had preceded him into the world and out of it.

54. 'The Chinaman' was a nickname given to HB by Angela Pietragrua, who thought he had Chinese eyes.

55. The reference is not to the mountain of Mont-Blanc, which rises to a height of 15,781 feet and would have been difficult to occupy, as well as being of more symbolic than strategic importance, but to the then *département* of Mont-Blanc.

56. These were both celebrated restaurants near the Palais-Royal, convenient for HB.

57. This was one of the great hits of the time, also referred to by E.T.A. Hoffmann: it comes from the opera by Niccolò Antonio Zingarelli, *Giulietta e Romeo*. Girolamo Crescentini was a great castrato; when Napoleon heard him sing in Vienna in 1805, the Emperor was so moved by his voice that he awarded him the Order of the Iron Crown of Lombardy.

58. Carpani had spoken of the young Haydn discovering the pleasures of the 'timpani', while Bombet has him discovering the allure of the 'tympanon', i.e. the dulcimer – admittedly an easy mistake to make. It is not clear how much Haydn liked the dulcimer, but he used the timpani to grand effect (the Nelson Mass, the introduction to *The Creation*, Symphony 103 'The Drumroll', etc.).

59. The mass must have been the 'Mass in Times of Trouble'.

60. An interesting point. Bach uses triple time to depict the solemn institution of the Eucharist in his St Matthew Passion, no doubt to make it seem like a Trinitarian dance.

61. A composer – or composers – whom HB rated highly.

62. We owe this tale to the fine story-teller Mérimée.

63. Others say it was on 25th July, somewhere else.

64. He must have reflected several times on the irony of the name of the restored dynasty: 'Bourbon' sounds so similar to *'bourbe'* = 'mud, mire'. When the Bourbons were restored to power in Naples after occupation by the French Republic, at the start of the nineteenth century, Cimarosa was sentenced to death; this was commuted to exile, which killed him (in Venice, 1801).

65. The event would have happened shortly after the battle of Bautzen. HB was accompanying a wagon train to Görlitz; it was attacked and nearly captured by Cossacks. HB apparently had to brief Napoleon about the skirmish in person.

66. There has been speculation that HB invented Byron's letter so that he could pen his indignant rejoinder (which was in turn apparently unfinished and thus probably never sent). HB claimed that, in Brescia, he had discussed Rossini's *Tancredi* with Pellico, 'the greatest tragic poet of Italy'. Pellico had found certain modulations shocking, but HB defended them: the ear sometimes needs to be surprised, he had said.

67. A Mrs Sarah Austin translated HB's French into English for publication in *The London Magazine*. HB wrote her a letter from Orléans, addressed to 'Mister Translator', giving her much useful advice on the practice of her art, and concluding with 'My wife is very well. Edgard sends his love.'

68. He nicknamed her 'Léonore'. No allusion to Beethoven's heroine Leonore, in *Fidelio*.

69. HB was probably referring to one of the Herodias paintings by Bernardino Luini.

70. Rossini's *Le Comte Ory* has recently been compared to an erection by a very prominent critic. These are things that Schenkerian analysis does not always bring out.

71. It gave its name to the painter Volterrano, who, as we have seen, induced an attack of Stendhal syndrome in HB.

72. His father died on 20th June 1819. HB paid little attention: he was obsessed by Metilde, and in any case 'the bastard' had left him little but debts. He had been ruined by investing in merino sheep during Napoleon's blockade of Europe which had kept English wool out of the continent. He too fell with Napoleon.

73. It is not clear whether HB is exaggerating here. Biographers cannot agree on how often he actually fell off his horse. Even the detailed study by the Count de Comminges, *Stendhal, homme de cheval* (Le Divan, 1928), which casts an informed and coolly professional eye on the question, does not entirely resolve the matter. (It has been claimed that the 'Comte de Comminges' is a pseudonym for Romain Colomb.) Of course, Lucien Leuwen in HB's novel of that name falls off his horse (twice) in front of Mme de Chasteller, and the important thing to note is that the *general theme* of falling (being unsteady on one's legs, as in an attack of 'Stendhal syndrome', or fainting from sheer fear and dread, as when Julien falls to the ground in front of the menacing Father Pirard) is one which HB associates with sensitivity.

74. Cf. the great love duet between Carlos and Posa in Verdi's *Don Carlos*.

75. The name 'Alexandrine' may have provoked deeper anxieties still in HB. 1) it was the name of the somewhat maternal Countess Daru with whom he had been in love; and 2) it was the name of the verse form that he had so singularly failed to master. Of course, 'Alexandrine' may have been a pseudonym.

76. It was translated into Danish by Johannes Martenssen, Professor of French Literature at the University of Copenhagen, and influenced the first generation of Kierkegaardians.

77. In the 1823 preface, HB wrote: 'So the present book is not a book' – largely because he had taken few pains to be strict about facts. Indeed, he had written this hotchpotch of unreliable anecdotes to provoke the composer into writing his own life. 'I hope that there will be a sufficient number of inaccuracies in this *Life of Rossini* to annoy him a little, and encourage him to write.'

78. These were the followers, not of the great seventeenth–eighteenth century writer the Duke de Saint-Simon, but of the nineteenth-century Saint-Simon who sang the praises of industrialism.

79. On discovering this *Review* – critical of the post-Congress of Vienna settlement, liberal, even Bonapartist at times, romantic and yet clear-headed – HB recognised, with some vexation (it was as if the *Review* had plagiarised

him!) some of his own most cherished beliefs and enthusiasms. He met many of his fellow contributors, notably Hazlitt.

80. The police chief looked back at HB's stay in Milan with indignation and alarm: 'Beyle, during his stay in Milan, which lasted several years, acquired a reputation as an irreligious, immoral and dangerous enemy of the legitimate powers, and it is thus incomprehensible that my predecessors could have tolerated him for so many years without making life difficult for him, especially given that he had the friendliest relations with our most notorious liberals.'

81. And Pellico was finally released from the Spielberg.

82. What if s/he was left-handed? Why would anyone want to profane the Host?

83. Historians have queried how many Jesuits actually took part in the street-fighting.

84. In this *Memorial*, Las Casas had noted down, day by day, on the grey island of South Atlantic exile, Napoleon's interminable *apologia pro vita sua*. HB thought it was 'a real **book** to read on the day before you are to be guillotined'.

85. This was Louis-Philippe.

86. In French: '*Esprit per. Pré. gui.* 11 A. 30'. This enigma was dragged out into the light of day by M. Parturier.

87. HB had the excellent therapeutic habit (which is sometimes claimed to be characteristic of women) of writing letters and not sending them. *The History of Painting in Italy* was summoned into being by a letter of advertisement that he jotted down in his diary and signed 'Is. Ich. Charlier', apparently destined for the newspapers but most probably a promissory note to himself to write the said work.

88. Freud thought that many-layered, eternally anachronistic Rome, in which all times seem to coexist, was a good image of the unconscious.

89. In his short story 'The Cenci' HB recounts how the ravishingly beautiful body of the executed Beatrice Cenci was brought to this church and buried in front of this very same painting. Raped by her father, she had collaborated in murdering him; she became a symbol of revolt against abusive aristocracy. Her burial was accompanied by all the Franciscan monks in Rome, and illuminated by fifty burning candles.

90. The bust in question seems actually to have been that of an anonymous man of the time of Hadrian.

91. In comparison with the grand remnants of antiquity, he thought, the arts of today were 'fucked, totally fucked'.

92. This is one of the most oddly touching visual traces of HB. John Adams ought to set this episode to music. Another memorial is the sculpture of his hands; HB posed (or lent a hand or two) to the statue of Mirabeau by Jean-Louis-Nicolas Jalley.

93. Actually, this was a little joke: Michelangelo is known as Michel-Ange in French, and the coffee machine in question had been brought back by one Michel-Ange Caetani.

94. William Carlos Williams, M.D., wrote poetry in between writing prescriptions. Sometimes he accidentally handed a poem to a patient, and sometimes what has been published as a poem is really a prescription.

95. The 'Dance of the Bee' captivated later French writers who really did see it, most notoriously Flaubert.

96. Reverend Elijah Parish Lovejoy (no relation) was the editor-in-chief of the abolitionist *Alton Observer*; he was shot dead by a mob of pro-slavery partisans on 7th November 1837.

97. For all his antiquarianism Mérimée – who also, of course, produced that *Beylist* work 'Carmen' – was not actually elected to the French Academy until 1844. HB owed him many things: without Mérimée, he might never have known the difference between the romanesque and gothic styles of architecture. HB may have influenced Mérimée's concision of style (or vice versa). But HB mocked Mérimée for starting to study Greek at the age of twenty-five. 'You're on the field of battle,' he said, 'you should be past the stage of polishing your rifle; now you need to shoot.'

98. Some Stendhal scholars claim that he was 'an able administrator', while others think he was negligent, lazy and irresponsible.

99. *Even his father* had been awarded the Legion of Honour! – HB too, much to his relief, was eventually granted this much-coveted decoration in 1835 – but he was annoyed to learn that he was being decorated, not for his talents as a soldier or a Consul, but for his *services to letters*. How dare they take his off-the-cuff fictions and travelogues seriously? And: how dare anyone think that a mere decoration could reward Literature?

100. It was not to become the capital of a united Italy until 1861, when it was still, *de facto*, part of the Papal States.

101. See in particular his study of the lovely Princess Albert de Broglie, née Joséphine-Éléonore-Marie-Pauline de Gallard de Brassac de Béarn, now in the Metropolitan Museum, New York.

102. The church of this particular unfortunate nun, Santa Maria della Vittoria, contains Bernini's statue of Saint Teresa in ecstasy, which has continued to inspire ideas of love both human and divine. Stendhal refers to it in his *Walks in Rome* (18th April 1828).

103. He had already protested to the *Courrier Français* about similar censorship in France, in 1822. On that occasion he signed himself 'a bookseller' (*un bouquiniste*).

104. He wrote several articles on the papal government and one on 'Rome and the Pope in 1832'.

105. He served the monarchy of Louis-Philippe with distinction until the revolution of 1848, when he declared himself to be a republican. One must move with the times.

106. He later savagely suppressed the 1871 Commune and was briefly head of state in the Third Republic.

107. There was a severe outbreak of cholera in 1835; Civitavecchia imposed strict quarantine on all visitors. HB noted the panic that spread throughout Italy; the common people were convinced that their governments were deliberately spreading the disease so as to get rid of undesirables (i.e. the common people).

108. It still is, of course; Parisians have happily abandoned the habit of renaming places in accordance with fluctuating political circumstances. *Tourisme oblige.* There is a fine restaurant in the Place de la République, which manages to square the ideological circle in a typically pragmatic way: it is called the 'Royal République'.

109. A will of 1832 had asserted that its author was dying 'in the bosom of the Church of Geneva' and 'in the Protestant Church of the Confession of Augsburg'. The Christian religion was so *geographical.*

110. Tavernier was a bit of a *'maniaque'* who clung to his desk and refused any life outside his job; like all good secretaries, he found himself correcting the careless oversights of his boss; his handwriting (*'Monsieur le Consul,* I have the honour to forward to you herewith an account of the cereals trade from 15th September to 1st October'; *'Monsieur le Consul,* I will do all in my power to send the fish to M. Constantin on Friday'; *'Monsieur le Consul,* yesterday evening I sent M. Constantin a fine fish weighing seven pounds and ten') was much more elegant than HB's impatient and almost horizontal scrawl. The relationship between this odd couple would make a good short novel.

111. i.e. the great seventeenth-century sceptic Pierre Bayle, viewed as a horrible heretic by the Catholic Church. The similarity between the names 'Bayle' and 'Beyle' almost certainly added to the suspiciousness with which the Apostolic Delegation in Civitavecchia viewed HB.

112. The word 'romance' might also refer to the novel or other fiction that he planned to write about this passion.

113. Some theologians have claimed that all contracts with God are necessarily of this kind.

114. (Latin): his John Thomas.

115. HB once almost fought a duel with a fan of Chateaubriand; the former had mocked Chateaubriand's lovely phrase 'the hazily swaying tree-tops'.

116. Bernardo Bertolucci's 1964 film *Before the Revolution* is a remarkable homage to *The Charterhouse of Parma.*

117. 'Prison'.

118. He had feared few things. Being killed in battle, hardly at all; ridicule, chronic illness, Pierre Daru much more. The repressive Austrian authorities

had caused him anxiety simply because they might keep him from his beloved Milan. Real terror he had felt, perhaps, only when approaching a second-floor apartment at no. 1175, Piazza Belgiojoso, Milan – the address of Metilde.

119. He had used it frequently in the rainy autumns of Rome.

120. Valerian Borowczyk adapted these *Walks* for his fascinating 1977 film *Inside A Convent*, with the lovely Ligia Branice, Marina Pierro and Gabriella Giacobbe as very special nuns.

121. This is really a mistranslation. *Souvenirs d'égotisme = Memories of Egotism* – not necessarily HB's own.

122. See his charming *hommage* to Raphael, the 'Virgin with the Fish', of 1818.

123. HB firmly believed this story, so it must be true.

Chronology

June: he is sent on a mission to Hungary.

October: Countess Daru, Pierre's wife, arrives in Vienna; HB starts to court her.

1810   January: he returns to Paris, and begins to study political economy.

1st August: he is appointed to a post as *auditeur* in the Conseil d'État (war department).

22nd August: he is appointed inspector of the Crown's furnishings and buildings, with special responsibility for the Palace of Fontainebleau and the inventorying of the *objets d'art* in the Musée Napoléon (i.e. the Louvre).

1811   HB travels to the Normandy coast and sees the sea for the first time.

August–November: he travels in Italy, as far south as Pompeii. In Milan he again meets Angela and declares his love. 'Why didn't you tell me back in 1801?' she asks him. He becomes (one of) her lover(s). He starts work on a history of painting in Italy.

1812   23rd July: he is ordered to leave for Russia on what he imagines will be an exciting jaunt.

September: he enters Moscow; the city is burned by the Russians; in October, together with the rest of the *Grande Armée*, he abandons the city. In November he is placed in charge of supplies for the army at Smolensk and ensures they get one of the few decent meals of the retreat. HB travels back to France via Königsberg, Danzig, Berlin, Frankfurt.

1813   31st January: HB arrives back in Paris.

April–May: he is *intendant* in Saga, Silesia. Struck down by a fever, he convalesces in Dresden.

September–November: still on sick leave, he visits Milan, and Angela Pietragrua. Their liaison turns stormy.

December: he is sent to aid the Count de Saint-Vallier in the defence of Grenoble against the Allied invasion.

1814   January–February: HB succumbs to overwork and depression.

February–March: he follows Saint-Vallier to Chambéry and then returns to Paris, which falls to the Allies. To take his mind off the fall of the Empire, he starts to put together his *Lives of Haydn etc.*

Summer: he decides to leave France rather than live under the Restoration.

10th August: he returns to Milan. He is penniless and in poor health; Angela's affection for him wavers. The next two years are dark and uncertain. He plunges into his history of Italian painting, and travels to Genoa, Leghorn, Florence (where he suffers an attack of Stendhal syndrome; the symptoms of this chronic illness never quite leave him), Bologna, and Parma.

1815   January, 'his' first book (*Lives of Haydn etc.*, mainly plagiarised from Carpani) is published under the *faux*-pompous name Louis-César-Alexandre Bombet. He is happy to have this work printed at his own expense even though he has no money and can hardly afford to eat. The book bombs at the booksellers. He reissues it in 1817. One of its small number of readers is an unhappy Carpani, who pursues 'Bombet' and finally manages, more or less, to pierce his incognito.

14th January: HB learns of the death of Countess Daru and writes on the cover of the manuscript of his *History of Painting in Italy*, 'To the everlasting memory of Milady Alexandra Z.' (his nickname for her).

5th March: he learns that Napoleon has escaped from Elba, but in spite of '**the most gay hopes of** success **for** Milan' (i.e. for Napoleon) decides not to gallop off to France to join him. He thus misses the 18th June Battle of Waterloo, at which Napoleon too is barely present (he is overwrought and suffering from piles; at one point, exhausted, he falls asleep).

25th July: HB learns the result of the Battle of Waterloo. The Congress of Vienna makes Napoleon's beautiful wife, Marie Louise, Duchess of Parma.

1816   HB's sister Pauline is left widowed (and ruined).

HB is still based in Milan, but in April–June is present in Grenoble and witnesses the bloody crushing of the so-called 'Didier conspiracy' against the restored monarchy. Some scholars have wondered why he was in Grenoble at just this time.

June–December: in Milan he attends La Scala and frequents the salons, becomes a friend of many liberals in the circle around Ludovico di Breme, meets the angelic, diabolical Byron, and becomes an enthusiastic reader of *The Edinburgh Review*. In December he visits Rome to study the Sistine Chapel frescoes for his *History of Painting in Italy*.

1817   September: publication, at his own expense, of *The History of Painting in Italy*, by 'M.B.A.A.' (Monsieur Beyle Ancien [Former] Auditeur).

1st–15th August: trip to London.

September: publishes *Rome, Naples and Florence in 1817*, using, for the first time in print, his *nom de plume* 'M. de Stendhal'.

November: returns from Paris to Milan with his sister Pauline; they are no longer so close, as HB finds her narrow-minded and provincial.

1818   HB works on a *Life of Napoleon* (unfinished). He is disappointed when a critic in his much-loved *Edinburgh Review* calls his *Rome,*

Naples and Florence 'flippant', and he continues to revise it. But he knows that his flippancy is worth ten times more than the '*sérieux*' of the pedants.

4th March: he falls in love with Metilde Dembowski. His unhappy passion for her coincides with his increasing engagement with liberal politics, and with the *querelle* of the romantics against the classicisers.

1819   Follows Metilde to Volterra, incognito, but is soon recognised.
20th June: death of Chérubin Beyle, aged seventy-two. HB travels to Grenoble to sort out his inheritance, only to discover that this consists essentially of debts.

December: Metilde is increasingly hostile to him; he decides to write a book about love.

1820   He sends the manuscript of *On Love* to Paris; it is lost in the post, and found only fourteen months later.

1821   There are uprisings in Piedmont and Naples; the Milan authorities crack down on dissidents (arrests, interrogations, imprisonments, exiles); life becomes increasingly difficult for HB, who – broken-hearted over Metilde's refusal to return his love – decides to leave Milan.

October–December: trip to London.

1822–30   HB frequents the salons of Paris and pursues the career of a man of letters. His broken heart has made him witty (he now has nothing to lose). He is given an entrée into some of the leading intellectual circles of the day; he writes columns for the English papers which provide a valuable account of French life under the Restoration.

1822   August: *On Love* published.

1823   March: *Racine and Shakespeare* published.
November: *Life of Rossini* published. Rossini has just come to live in Paris and is infuriated.

1824   May: Countess Clémentine Curial becomes his mistress. They have a stormy liaison. HB continues his career as a journalist, writing for the *Journal de Paris* on art and music.

1825   1st May: Metilde dies in Milan.
December: HB publishes his pamphlet *On a new plot against industrialists*, which criticises the contemporary vogue for technocratic solutions and dismisses the cult of mere productivity. It is a work of considerable importance, expressing HB's hostility to the work ethic, to the catastrophic effects of the Industrial Revolution, to exploitation and domination, etc.

1826   June: following his break-up with Clémentine, HB embarks on a new trip to England (as far north as Newcastle).

1827	Trip to Italy (Genoa, Leghorn, Elba, Naples, Ischia, Rome, Naples, Venice).

1827   Trip to Italy (Genoa, Leghorn, Elba, Naples, Ischia, Rome, Naples, Venice).

August: HB publishes (anonymously, at the age of forty-four) his first novel, or rather the first work that he labels as such: *Armance*.

1828   1st–2nd January: HB arrives in Milan and is ordered by the Austrian authorities to leave within twelve hours. He is again broke, and looking for a job. In October this year, his *bête noire* Chateaubriand arrives in Rome to take up his position as French Ambassador (but soon resigns).

1829   HB would like a position as librarian at the Royal Library, but his application is turned down.

June: Alberthe de Rubempré becomes his mistress. She is an excellent lover; he demonstrates that he is no Octave (the flagging anti-hero of *Armance*). But she is repeatedly unfaithful, and the liaison rapidly becomes stormy.

September: publication of *Walks in Rome*.

September–November: travels in southern France (Bordeaux, Toulouse, Carcassonne, Montpellier, Grenoble, Marseille) and Barcelona.

1830   8th April: HB signs, for the first time, a proper contract with a publisher, for *The Red and the Black*.

29th July: HB watches the Revolution from a safe distance, and spends the night with his current mistress, Giulia Rinieri, who is scared by the upheaval.

25th September: HB's attempts to be appointed to a Prefecture have failed, but he is given the post of Consul at Trieste.

6th November: HB asks for Giulia's hand in marriage, but her guardian refuses. He leaves for Trieste.

November: publication of *The Red and the Black*.

24th December: he is informed that the Austrian government will not allow him to take up his post in Trieste.

1831–42   HB is appointed Consul in Civitavecchia. This is his last job; in several respects his life will change little from now on. He spends as much time in Rome as he can, or in Naples, or Florence, or Tuscany, or Paris, leaving the consulate in the capable hands of Lysimaque Caftangi-Oglou Tavernier. He becomes interested in archaeology; he discovers, in Rome, manuscripts from or about Renaissance Italy that provide the kernel for several late fictions, he starts novels (*A Social Position*, *Lucien Leuwen*) which he never finishes, since he feels too old for that kind of thing, and autobiographical works (*Memoirs of an Egotist*, *The Life of Henry Brulard*) which he also leaves unfinished, since no autobiography can ever be completed.

1835   The Legion of Honour!

1836   He leaves Civitavecchia for Paris, and manages to ensure that his
        leave lasts for three years.

1837–8 He travels widely: Brittany, the Dauphiné, Southern France –
        and from his travels derives the *Memoirs of a Tourist* (1838). Then
        Germany, Holland and Belgium.

1839   April: publication of *The Charterhouse of Parma*.
        10 August: returns to Civitavecchia.

1840   The '**last romance**', with 'Earline'.
        25th September: rave review of *The Charterhouse of Parma*, by
        Balzac.

1841   15th March: HB suffers from an apoplectic attack – a 'tussle with
        oblivion'.
        21st October: HB takes sick leave from Civitavecchia and travels
        to Paris.

1842   22nd March, at 7 p.m., HB suffers from an attack of apoplexy in
        the rue Neuve-des-Capucines. He dies at two o'clock the next
        morning, still unconscious.

1847   Napoleon's lovely widow, Marie Louise, since 1815 an intelligent,
        liberal and reforming Duchess of Parma, dies. She had been forced
        to abdicate by social unrest in her realms; she is duly mourned
        by all her subjects. Parma's liberal credentials are embellished by
        the fact that it is the birthplace of Verdi and Toscanini; and later,
        in 1922, during Mussolini's march on Rome, Parma alone among
        the cities of Emilia resists the Fascists.

1848   The 'Springtime of Peoples'; barricades are erected across Europe,
        and uprisings against authoritarian regimes in Austria, Hungary,
        the German States, Prussia, Venice, Turin, Rome, and Milan
        show the world that, after so many years, Julien Sorel and the
        silkworkers of Lyon have worthy successors. In France, the
        Second Republic declares universal suffrage, abolishes slavery,
        and appoints artists and intellectuals to key government positions.
        The prisons of Paris are empty.

1935   Stendhal's work is still being read. He has won the lottery!

1936   In May, the Popular Front wins the elections in France. Its leader,
        Léon Blum, is the author of an important study of Stendhal. Faced
        with the rise of fascism, Blum's government decrees two weeks'
        paid holidays for French workers. (The rise of modern *tourism*
        dates from this period in France.)

3805   Stendhal's work is still being read – as he had once hoped.

Some of HB's maxims (reported by Mérimée):

'Until he's thirty, a man who happens to be alone with a woman should always try his chances with her. He has a one-in-ten chance of succeeding: it's well worth the risk.'

'You should enter a salon like the statue of the Commendatore.'

'When you go into society for the first time, seize the opportunity of having a quarrel.'

'While your opponent [in a duel] is taking aim at you, look at a tree, and apply yourself to counting its leaves.'

Bibliography

I have used several biographies of Stendhal, including these excellent works:

Robert Alter, in collaboration with Carol Cosman, *Stendhal: a biography* (London: Allen and Unwin, 1980);
Jonathan Keates, *Stendhal* (London: Minerva, 1995);
and Michel Crouzet, *Stendhal, ou, Monsieur Moi-même* (Paris: Flammarion, 1990).

I have also spent much happy time browsing the *Dictionnaire de Stendhal*, ed. Yves Ansel, Philippe Berthier and Michael Nerlich (Paris: H. Champion, 2003).

But I have drawn mainly on Stendhal's own letters and diaries, available in several editions, including the charming (but editorially outdated) 16-cm 'Le Divan' edition of 1927–1937 (ed. Henri Martineau), as well as in more recent editions published in the 'Bibliothèque de la Pléiade' or (for the letters) the *Correspondance générale* edited by Victor del Litto (Paris: H. Champion, 1997–9).

The best introduction to Stendhal is Léon Blum, *Stendhal et le beylisme*, 3rd edn (Paris: A. Michel, 1947). Unfortunately it seems never to have been translated into English.

Apart from the films already mentioned, Kenji Mizoguchi's *The Lady of Musashino* (1951) shows how destructive the influence of Stendhal can be if he is read *too egotistically*.

Acknowledgments

Thanks to Alice, who read a first draft of this at a time when her mind was on much more exciting things, and to Ellie, who commented with exactitude and forbearance. Corinne supplied me with books and good humour. Étienne kindly allowed me to quote from his forthcoming study of utopias. Ivano di Lillo and Carla dalla Noce provided me with information about Stendhal's current reputation in the Milanese peninsula.

Any remaining faults are due to vanity (as Étienne pointed out, beylefully).